X 56

LR

CLIO AMONG THE MUSES

Bill Olbrich
Temple, TX
October 2020

Clio among the Muses

Essays on History and the Humanities

Peter Charles Hoffer

NEW YORK UNIVERSITY PRESS
New York and London

NEW YORK UNIVERSITY PRESS
New York and London
www.nyupress.org

Library of Congress Cataloging-in-Publication Data
Hoffer, Peter Charles, 1944–
Clio among the muses : essays on history and the humanities / Peter Charles Hoffer.
pages cm   Includes bibliographical references and index.
ISBN 978-1-4798-3283-5 (hardback)
1. History—Methodology. 2. Historiography. 3. History—Philosophy.
4. Humanities. I. Title.
D16.H686   2013
907.2—dc23   2013027458

CONTENTS

PREFACE

In beginning our history proper, it might perhaps be wise to
forget all that we have said before and start fresh, as a lot of
new things have come up.

ROBERT BENCHLEY, 1944

The humorist, essayist, and pseudo-documentary movie maker Robert
Benchley had a rare gift for parody. One of his targets was the academic
know-it-all who learns everything from books. For example, "in order
to write about snake-charming, one has to know a little about its history,
and where should one go to find out about history but to a book. Maybe
in that pile of books in the corner is one on snake-charming. Nobody
could point the finger of scorn at me if I went over to those books for the
avowed purpose of research work."

Benchley put his finger on exactly what historians do when they write
about other historians (a subject inelegantly called "historiography"). They
go over to that pile of books, sort and read, compile genealogies of ideas
and methods, and make judgments, and another book goes on top of the
pile. Historians (if not, alas, their readers) find the study of the discipline
of history endlessly fascinating. For at the center of the study of the past is
a compelling paradox: We demand to know about the past but can never
be sure we have gotten our account right. We would love to go back in time
(all historians are secret re-enactors), but we cannot go back, and even if
we could, how could we see all the events from all the perspectives that the
past offers? History is Odysseus' Sirens calling us to a place that we cannot
reach, yet we persist in listening. The Sirens' call is so enchanting—writing

history is an act of such artistry—who can blame historians for spending a lifetime of research and writing at their command?

In a 1998 essay for the American Historical Association's *Perspectives*, the historian Peter N. Stearns listed the benefits of studying history: History helps us understand change, provides clues to our own identity, and hones our moral sense. But history is not a standalone discipline. Indeed, it stands on the shoulders of its companions in the humanities and social sciences. In the following pages' brief span, I assay history's complicated partnership with its coordinate disciplines of religion, philosophy, social science, literature, biography, policy studies, and law. These are Clio's modern sister disciplines, comparable to the eight other muses who accompanied Clio in the ancient world. That companionship, sometimes immensely rewarding, sometimes testy and rancorous, adds to the authority and humanity of chronicle, but history is not just the accumulation of other disciplines' knowledge. More than the sum of these collaborations, the study of history is something unique, ennobling, and necessary. One can live without religion, philosophy, and the rest. One cannot exist without history. But I do not want to give away here what should be earned by reading the following pages.

I wish to acknowledge those kind people who have assisted me in this Herculean task (which I liken to wrestling Antaeus): Clive Priddle and Michael McGandy for their help in my attempts to grapple with the meaning and method of history; Peter Onuf and Claire Potter, whose readings of an earlier essay taught me how to get a hold on key themes; and Richard Bernstein, William Cronon, Paul Finkelman, Michael Gagnon, John T. Juricek, Stanley Katz, Allan Kulikoff, Maureen Nutting, Thomas Whigham, and Michael Winship, whose combined intellectual weight added to my own effort enabled me to pin down the subject. Michael Zuckerman's refereeing of the manuscript was overly kind, his pages of admonitions and emendations invariably fair. My wife and scholarly partner, N. E. H. Hull, and my older son, Williamjames Hull Hoffer, have read bits and pieces of this project over a course of years and cheered me on. At New York University Press, editor Debbie Gershenowitz urged me to submit the manuscript; and her successor editor, Clara Platter, guided it through the Press Board approval process and then offered a remarkably kind pre-edit. No wrestling match with an opponent as experienced and wily as history will ever result in a complete victory, but to all of the kind people who shared this contest with me, my heartfelt thank you.

Introduction

The Problem with History

It is said that Clio cannot be taken by storm, but requires
much patient and skillful Wooing. Moreover, Clio likes a certain degree of self-effacement in her suitors.

> CHARLES DOWNER HAZEN,
> "This Country as Mr. Chesterton Sees It,"
> *New York Times Book Review*, June 8, 1919

Clio, paramount among the nine ancient Greek muses, was gifted by
her mother with memory and shared lyric skills with her eight sisters.
She inspired those who assayed to sing, tell, and write stories of the past.
Ancient audiences held the followers of Clio in high regard, for they
captured the imagination of the listener and reader. For Hellenes gathered around the fire pit to hear Homer sing about Troy, or Hellenized
Romans who delighted in reading their copy of Plutarch's *Parallel Lives*,
or the monks in the English abbeys who squinted in the candlelight as
they re-read older chronicles of the lives of Saxon saints and kings, or
the thousands of nineteenth-century middle-class families that gathered
in gaslit parlors to devour the tales of heroism in Francis Parkman's volumes, history enchanted and instructed, just as Clio wished. The Greeks
defeated the Trojans; Caesar failed where Alexander the Great succeeded;
Alfred the Great unified Anglo-Saxon England; and the British chased
the French and their Indian allies from North America for reasons that

historians' listeners and readers thought worth knowing. In the nine-teenth century, no educated person in the West doubted that history was "assigned the office of judging the past, of instructing the present for the benefit of future ages."[1]

The university-trained historians of the late nineteenth century echoed this creed as they lobbied for required history courses in the schools alongside the sciences.

> If it is desirable that the high-school pupil should know the physical world, that he should know the habits of ants and bees, the laws of floral growth, the simple reactions in the chemical retort, it is certainly even more desir-able that he should be led to see the steps in the development of the human race, and should have some dim perception of his own place, and of his country's place, in the great movements of men. . . . All our institutions, our habits of thought and modes of action, are inheritances from preced-ing ages: no conscious advance, no worthy reform, can be secured without both a knowledge of the present and an appreciation of how forces have worked in the social and political organization of former times.

Historians and teachers of history wanted everyone to be able to judge history and assumed the value of such judgment. In a "best practices" piece for the American Historical Association (AHA), Peter Stearns warned, "In the past[,] history has been justified for reasons we would no longer accept," but taught well, history still had the power to delight, instruct, and empower.[2]

Sadly, Clio's enticements faded as war and genocide in the twentieth century turned history into a horror story. The ease with which cynical and maniacal political leaders and their ideological abetters used history to justify their policies of conquest and annihilation drove Clio from her pedestal. In "the bloodbath of European fighting in the First World War and the Second World War, the Holocaust, and the present threat to environmental resources," who could trust the old ideas of beauty, prog-ress, reason, and education the histories once proclaimed? There was too much history for us to bear. "For as long as we can discern, the past has loomed ominously above the lives of men, threatening, demanding, and hinting at cataclysm. . . . Its dark firmament has glittered with examples, a few benevolent, most doom laden. Embedded in this mass of belief, which fulfilled, as we shall see, diverse and necessary social purposes, were bits and pieces of truth." Historians were shaken; their faith "that they could understand by a simple process of induction the forces that shaped the past now seemed dangerously naïve."[3]

Weary and wary academics now warn that the student of history will suffer "bitter disappointment" if he or she seeks guidance from history. A bestselling textbook in philosophy of history issued the following warning: "Historians are not the guardians of universal values, nor can they deliver 'the verdict of history.'" A popular history of historical writing summed up this judgment: "[A]lways handle history with care." Even defenses of the historical profession today begin with a *mea culpa*: "We professors," as American Historical Association President Anthony Grafton ruefully recounted the "barrage" of charges against history, "are imprisoned within sclerotic disciplines, obsessed with highly specialized research. We can't write except in meaningless jargon, and we address only esoteric students, thus insuring that we have no audience." Not surprising, then, that Keith Jenkins, the *enfant terrible* of philosophy of history, found the search for the truth in history an "unachievable" goal, misleading at best, for "the truths of the past elude us. . . . [H]istory is intersubjective and ideologically positioned, objectivity and being unbiased are chimeras." This much is certain—truths that once seemed within our reach are now beyond our grasp.[4]

The pervasive disenchantment of the academics echoed popular perceptions of the futility of historical study. Entertaining though it might be, it was still "the bunk," "lie," and "one damn thing after another." What the popular mind especially rejected was the uniqueness and authority of historical study. A popular essay on the meaning of the past at the end of the twentieth century by a nonhistorian, Francis Fukuyama, reduced history to a Swiss Army knife whose many attachments one can manipulate to fit any need, useful because they are so conveniently manipulated. Forget the claims of the professional historian to objectivity. "Just as a modern economist does not try to define a product's 'utility' or 'value' in itself, but rather accepts the marketplace's valuation of it as expressed in a price, so one would accept the judgment of the marketplace of world history." In that process, "we can think of human history as a dialogue or competition between different regimes or forms of social organization." In other words, we could buy and sell histories—the perfect fit for a consumer-driven intellectual marketplace—with the result that some academic historians have morphed into consulting editors and staff writers for mass-market magazines.[5]

The distrust of the academic historians and their work product exploded in the last years of the twentieth century, when the National Endowment for the Humanities underwrote a study of history lesson plans for secondary schools. At the head of the project was a professor of history at UCLA, and other academics sat on various drafting committees. Finished and published in 1994, the *National History Standards* draft curriculum for K–12 seemed to be a little short on heroes and far too long on slavery, violence, and other blemishes in American history. Conservative critics of the suggested "student achievement examples" were appalled. Lynne Cheney, who as chairperson of the National Endowment for the Humanities during President George H.W. Bush's administration had sponsored the project, later recalled that the *National History Standards* "reflected the gloomy, politically driven revisionism" that had become "all too familiar on college campuses." George Washington, U. S. Grant, and Robert E. Lee were gone, replaced by women of color, labor radicals, and other minor figures. Enduring values were gone too; only oppression remained. On October 20, 1994, Cheney's op-ed piece "The End of History" graced the back pages of the *Wall Street Journal*. In it, she ridiculed the project for elevating the National Organization for Women, the Sierra Club, and Harriet Tubman in importance above the Constitution, the U.S. Congress, and the Civil War. The result was a "grim and gloomy" account of America that could give comfort to only the "politically correct" (as if the Revolution and the Civil War did not have some grim and gloomy moments).[6]

Repeating Henry Ford's infamous dismissal of all history, then-Congressman Newt Gingrich aimed his fire at the professional historians: "[T]he fiasco over the American and Western history standards is a reflection of what has happened to the world of academic history. The profession and the American Historical Association are now dominated by younger historians with a familiar agenda: Take the west down a peg, romanticize 'the Other' (non-whites), treat all cultures as equal, refrain from criticizing non-white cultures." The *National History Standards* was condemned in a 99–1 U.S. Senate vote.[7]

The chair of the drafting committee, UCLA history professor Gary Nash, defended the document and the process by which it had been created. He later recalled, "Those who were at first reluctant about the wisdom of this enterprise soon decided that they might compromise their own best interests if they failed to join in. If the cards were being dealt, why would historians or social studies educators not want seats around the big table?" The process was long and arduous but uplifting. "Never in the long history of public education, reaching back more than three hundred years, had such an attempt been made to raise the level of history education. Never before had such a broad-based group of history educators from all parts of the country gathered to work collaboratively on such an enterprise. The History Standards Project represented the building of bridges between two groups of largely separated educators. These bridges may even outlast the standards themselves." But the controversy was not really about the standards. It was about the uses of history. "The history standards controversy laid bare competing meanings of patriotism and the question of how to inculcate the ideal of citizenship in young students. For the Cheney-led cohort, children who learn about the Ku Klux Klan and McCarthyism will not learn to love their country. It will embarrass and make cynics of them. For historians, the approach favored by critics is sugar-coated history that will make cynics of children because they will grow up to find that the bland or celebratory history books have excluded or misrepresented the realities of past life."[8]

Nash was waging an uphill battle, not only against those who disputed his expertise and the cachet that expertise supposedly brought but also against those who saw in history proof of our inability to know the past with certainty. We yearn for the comforting past, for as the celebrated literary critic Frank Kermode wrote shortly before he passed away, "[W]e project our existential anxieties on to history." It was for this very reason that during the bitter partisan contests of the 1820s, the surviving founding fathers feared that Americans would forget the sacrifices of previous generations. Shortly before he died, Thomas Jefferson wrote to his longtime friend James Madison, "It has also been a great solace to me to believe that you are engaged in vindicating to posterity the course we have pursued. . . . [T]ake care of me when [I am] dead." Our political leaders still want to get right with history, particularly when the verdict of history is uncertain. At his farewell press conference on January 11, 2009, outgoing President George W. Bush expressed the hope that "History will be the judge. . . . History will look back and determine" whether he had failed in his trust or left the world a better, safer place than he had found it. President Bush compared himself to Lincoln, two wartime presidents burdened with history. So the problem facing the student of history is how to woo Clio, how to sustain an arguable case that the historians' methods for knowing about the past are as valid as any other way of knowing about the past. As my first history teacher, Hayden White, wrote in 1966, "[T]he burden of the historian in our time is to reestablish the dignity of historical studies."[9]

As this very brief tour of "the problem" with history reveals, history has a history, a changing cast of chroniclers working in a varied collection of institutions, sharing a vital concern about the meaning of the past. Along the way, the doing of history has evolved in a convoluted fashion from storytelling and soothsaying to its recognizable modern form. Although popular historians and academic historians may not always use the same methods, they share a place in the history of history with religious writers, philosophers, social scientists, men and women of letters, biographers, policy makers, and lawgivers who use history. It is this story—the story of history and its related disciplines—that I want to tell here.

It may seem, as one reads the following pages, that my project resembles Stephen Leacock's impetuous nobleman who flings "himself upon his horse and rides madly off in all directions," but there is a method to the organization of this book. While the outer frame—the seven chapters—is topical, the order of the topics reflects the chronological order of history's encounter with each chapter's subject matter. History and religion were born together. Philosophy made its claim on history in the classical period of Western civilization. In the seventeenth century, the introduction of the social sciences added another member to Clio's modern family. The eighteenth century imposed literary canons on the historian. The next century's celebration of the great man drew biography and history together. The twentieth century's near-fatal fascination with war gave rise to historically infused policy studies. In the closing decades of the twentieth century and the opening years of the twenty-first century, the explosion of historical consulting and expert witnessing in law cases made history and law close collaborators.[10]

Not only are the chapters arrayed in chronological order, within each chapter my account is roughly chronological. Each chapter thus stands on its own, a story of collaboration and rivalry, of cross-fertilization and competition, like the story of any family. Though they sometimes squabble, Clio and her companions are inseparable. On the foundation of this comparative approach, we can see the particular strengths of the historical way of knowing and determine if, in the final analysis, the entire enterprise of historical scholarship is worth our investment in it. If history is "a pool, sometimes benign, sometimes sulfurous, that lies under the present, silently shaping our institutions, our ways of thought, our likes and our dislikes" that "we call on for validation, and for lessons and advice," an inquiry into the validity of historical judgment is a vital intellectual task not just for the historian, but for anyone who reads history and takes it seriously.[11]

A final, more personal confession: Like so many other academics, I was guilty of the Baconian fallacy of wanting to know everything about this subject before I wrote anything. For years, I amassed file boxes of note cards, certain that just a few more forays into the library would sate the muse. But self-indulgence was a trap, and the longer I held off writing the closer I came to "giv[ing] up [my] soul to weariness and resignation." My escape from this snare was to adopt what I have come to call the synecdochal method—not exactly sampling, but using selected parts to represent the whole. I focused on the critical moments when history and its companions were in genuine conversation. Some examples: I elected to devote most of the first chapter on history and religion to the encounter between Judeo-Christian chronology and Western science because Judaism and Christianity are particularly concerned with history, and modern science questions traditional Judeo-Christian views of history. In the third chapter, on history and the social sciences, I focus much of my attention on the half-century between 1875 and 1925 because that was the period when social science and history most closely paralleled each other. In chapter 6, on history and policy studies, I focused on warfare because my concern was to show the crucial interaction of the two disciplines rather than explore every place where they might interact. By selecting portions of the long dialogue between history and its companions rather than tracking the entirety of the conversation, I found I could illuminate my thesis without blinding the reader. A more universally knowledgeable scholar would have included more examples, but a truly encyclopedic work, like the Moiré pattern that appears when an electronic image is overly enlarged, would have resulted in a pattern of black dots rather than a recognizable picture.[12]

[1]

History and Religion

The holy spirit of God writes in an open book this sacred
history which is not yet finished nor will be till the end of the
world. This history contains an account of the guidance and
designs of God with regard to men.

JOHN-PIERRE DE CAUSSADE, *Abandonment to*
Divine Providence (1673)

Religion is both history's foremost rival and first aegis. The result is an
uneasy collaboration. The earliest surviving invocations of priests and religious mystics include references to history. With these words the intimate
tie of history and religion is written and sealed—that is, if history is God's
work and our study of history a search for the details of God's decree. Even
for the skeptic, the impulse behind religion—to find the deeper meaning
of the spirit—is never far from the motivating force behind the study of
history. Religion and history are prickly but avowed partners in this quest.

I have a colleague who teaches and writes about religious history. He
is not a believer. But when he unravels the conversations among the
Puritans he enters into their world so totally that the question of his own
beliefs fades into the background. He becomes one of them. Watching
his career and reading his work convinces me that one need not take a
position on religion itself to understand how closely tied religion and
history, religious studies and historical studies, are. I am not a believer
in divine plans, intervention, or supervision of human conduct, but I do
believe that history and religion are indissolubly tied.[1]

A Very Brief and Highly Eclectic History of Religious Histories

Once upon a time, written history and religious writings were inseparable. They shared a birthright. The priests of yore were the first historians. Religious texts passed from hand to hand, the work of "untold generations of scribes." Mayan glyphs, the historical records of kings and battles, were also the record of religious observances. The Tanakh is a history of the human race in general and the origins of Judaism suffused with the presence of Hashem. The histories of Saxon England were the work of monks as were the histories of the Celts. Medieval chroniclers were clerics. One could multiply the list, but the point is undeniable. The documentation of human events and the recording of religious beliefs had a common ancestry.[2]

The religiously based histories with which Western culture is familiar had a linear narrative form. Time begins at creation and continues through judgment. An immanent God, with whom Abraham had covenanted, who allowed his only begotten son to suffer for mankind's sins, watches over His people. Modern eyes see in Bible the influences of the time and place on its authors. Historians call this "context." The end of the Jewish Bible is coincident with the return of the Jewish people from their Babylonian exile about 515 B.C.E. That is when the books of the Bible were reduced to writing on animal skins by scribes. The Babylonians had their own origin or creation story, the Enuma Elish, and its beginning bears a strong similarity to Genesis. For the Jews and their former Babylonian captors, creation was the beginning of time. God or the gods create the earth, the waters, and time itself. Man occupies the space, honors God or the gods, and begins his travails.

Other religions see history traveling in cycles. The world-cycle of the stoic is an endless repetition that one can retell but cannot change. For the Hindu, in the beginning of the cycle, the world is new and fresh, a flower that is budding. At the end of the cycle, bad events presage a terrible calamity. Like the seasons, the world dies and is reborn. History is the record of events in these cycles and, read correctly, predicts each stage of rise and decay. In each cycle, forms of worship may change, for worship is human in origin, "with socioeconomic, political, historical, or climatic causes."

These link the religious cycle to "historically significant events" that must be chronicled if one is to understand the inner workings of the cycle itself.[3]

The oldest creation stories are not for the squeamish. Society and culture come into being rough-hewn. Native Americans' origin stories recalled warring siblings, untrustworthy spirits, malevolent animals, and ignorant people. The Aztec creation story, tied to the agricultural cycle, ran through a series of bloody sacrifices. Every year an "impersonator" of the creation deity Tezcatlipoca, a figure of strife and darkness, lost his life in a ritual of bloodletting. In the Tanakh the Jewish people inflict suffering on one another and take revenge on their enemies. Whole cities vanish as punishment for their perfidy.

In the later nineteenth and early twentieth centuries, students of religion and students of history embarked on a common (though not collaborative) effort to determine how accurate religious depictions of human history origins were. This hermeneutic quest led some historians to conclude that the religious stories were mythological. The theologians decided that the historians missed the spiritual significance of texts. The effort failed. But easily dismissed by modern humanists as themes and variations on mythology, in fact the various creation stories recapitulated essential historical events—the conquests of one people by another, floods, volcanic eruptions, earthquakes, migrations, and the rise of new cults. While the keepers of these distant memories did not subject them to source criticism, bound into religious observances they kept alive a history that could not have otherwise survived.[4]

While modern critical scholarship subjects religious stories to judgments external to the particular religious tradition itself, the first religious historians took the job seriously because they believed they saw the guiding hand of the deity in all history. Like their work, they would be judged wanting if it were found wanting. Human events perceived by human eyes and chronicled by human hands were imperfect records of the deity's design, to be sure, making the confidence of these chroniclers suspect. But history was to them a proof of Providence, and in the course of human events one found clues to God's intentions for men and women.

In a sense, this history was partisan. It served a cause. It also had moral implications, though these might be contradictory. Sometimes it spurred men to violent acts in the name of the true faith. Sometimes it served to remind men who were hell-bent on violence that there was a final judgment. Consider the case of some of the Frankish kings, successors to the Roman magistrates of Gaul, who had little regard for Christian virtues, including hospitality. Their impious attitude spurred Gregory, bishop of the Frankish Roman city of Tours in the sixth century, to write their history.

> Proposing as I do to describe the wars waged by kings against hostile peoples, by martyrs against the heathen, and by Churches against the heretics, I wish first of all to explain my own faith. . . . My one desire is that, without the slightest deviation, and with no hesitation whatsoever in my heart, I may hold fast to what is ordained in church that we should believe, for I know that one given to sin may obtain pardon with God through the purity of his faith.

The Franks, whose kings were as brutal and corrupt as any (especially to their kinfolk), might appear to be a proof that God had turned his eyes away from the successor kingdoms to the Roman Empire, but Gregory could not tell their story without a faith in God's ultimate sway and the vital role of the Church in history.[5]

As Christianity spread to the far corners of Europe, religious chroniclers found the hand of the deity in the most unexpected places. In the eighth century, the "Venerable" Bede, a northern English monk, crafted one of the most respected of all Christian histories. The conversion story of St. Alban was typical of Bede's lessons: "When infidel rulers [in England] were issuing violent edicts against the Christians, Alban, though still a heathen at the time, gave hospitality to a certain cleric who was fleeing from his persecutors. When Alban saw this man occupied day and night in continual vigils and prayers, divine grace suddenly shown upon him, and he learned to imitate his guests' faith and devotion. . . . Alban forsook the darkness of idolatry and became a wholehearted Christian."

Alban would martyr himself to protect the stranger and their common faith, and his fate remained an example of history's teaching God's will.[6]

Later Middle Age kings and their vassals ranged over the Flemish countryside in Jean Froissart's chronicles of the years 1327–1400. Though devoted to battles, sieges, and the lives of knights, the work remains profoundly religious. "God, who is all seeing and all powerful" lurked backstage throughout the work, for "if god is good to us in the battle" the virtuous would win and the villainous fail. For in the end, men's guile and strength could not prevail in an unjust cause. God stood behind the victors. How could it be otherwise?[7]

No group of people was more committed to the historical search for signs of God's will than the English radical religious reform party called "hot blooded puritans" by their critics. The Puritans in seventeenth-century New England saw themselves as a people chosen by God whose mission to the New World history would vindicate, and they looked to history to prove their point. Edward Johnson's *Wonder-Working Providence of Sion's Saviour In New-England* (1654) applied this reading of God's plan to the Puritans' historical experience—"the working providence of Christ to stir up this English nation, to plant these parts" as the Lord had bid the Israelites depart the corruptions of Egyptian bondage. The Lord spread disease through the native peoples to clear the land for His chosen people. Surviving Indians were God's instruments to aid the settlement. Each success was a remarkable proof of favoring Providence. Each setback was God's test of the Puritans' will. The history the Puritans wrote was proof of God's plan for His chosen people in New England.[8]

In the nineteenth-century United States, religion and history still found each other to be companions. The puritan ideal of history, reaching vertically from believer up to the Lord, was laid on its side and made a justification for western expansion. Typically, the Democratic publicist John O'Sullivan explained the need for westward migration in historical and religious terms.

We must onward to the fulfilment of our mission—to the entire development of the principle of our organization—freedom of conscience, freedom of person, freedom of trade and business pursuits, universality of freedom and equality. This is our high destiny, and in nature's eternal, inevitable decree of cause and effect we must accomplish it. All this will be our future history, to establish on earth the moral dignity and salvation of man—the immutable truth and beneficence of God.

The doctrine was called "manifest destiny," for history and God together had ordained it. In the Civil War, both sides appealed to history and to God for inspiration. As Abraham Lincoln said in his second inaugural address,

Neither party expected for the war the magnitude or the duration which it has already attained. Neither anticipated that the cause of the conflict might cease with, or even before, the conflict itself should cease. Each looked for an easier triumph, and a result less fundamental and astounding. Both read the same Bible, and pray to the same God; and each invokes his aid against the other. It may seem strange that any men should dare to ask a just God's assistance in wringing their bread from the sweat of other men's faces; but let us judge not, that we be not judged. The prayers of both could not be answered—that of neither has been answered fully.[9]

The quest for religious meaning in past events proceeds apace today among those who believe in an immanent deity. They maintain one cannot simply say that natural catastrophes and man's inhumanity to man have no meaning, that they just are. "We must go beyond theses pragmatic, realist reasons to reject the call for silence. It is erroneous. Scripture teaches that God directs the course of events so as to give meaning to history. However difficult it often is for us to discern that meaning." To be sure, the "must" here is less a scholarly one than part of the search for the nature of God.[10]

This religious version of global history one might call "the new ecumenical history." If one were to put aside the "Eurocentrism" of much of Western history (maps with Europe at their center; accounts of "civilization" that begin with Aristotle and end with Western science; meta-narratives that explain why imperialism was good for the colonies) and focus instead on the common spiritual yearnings of all peoples, one could fashion a "trans-cultural" spiritual history. Perhaps this is what the Second Vatican Council's Declaration "*Dignitatis Humanae*, on the Right of the Person and of Communities to Social and Religious Freedom in Matters Religion" aspired to promote. Certainly, the core of that Declaration, that "A sense of the dignity of the human person has been impressing itself more and more deeply on the consciousness of contemporary man, and the demand is increasingly made that men should act on their own judgment, enjoying and making use of a responsible freedom," lends itself to an ecumenical view of history.

It is the hope of ecumenicists that one can interpret human acts in human terms within a larger framework of shared religious values. As the medieval Jewish philosopher and theologian Moses Maimonides wrote, "[D]o not imagine that character is determined at birth. We have been given free will. Any person can become as righteous as Moses or as wicked as Jeroboam. We ourselves decide whether to make ourselves learned or ignorant, compassionate or cruel, generous or miserly. No one forces us, no one decides for us, no one drags us along one path or the other; we ourselves, by our own volition, choose our own way."[11]

But what if one were to tell another story about the meaning of history? What if that story denied the role of religion entirely? What if it saw religion, at least implicitly, as a pervasive misrepresentation of the course of history? Such a story exists; indeed, it is the central story of the modern science of creation.

The Challenge of Evolution

The most devastating critique of religious views of history comes not from the historical profession but from evolutionary biology. The evolution of species is a historical account of the earth's biological history that directly confutes religious eschatology. The history of that concept is worth recounting. In 1859, after more than twenty years of cautious inquiry, Charles Darwin published *On the Origin of Species*. At its heart was an idea of how new species evolved from older ones. Darwin rushed into print because other biologists, notably Alfred Russel Wallace and Richard Owen, were hot on the trail of the same idea, but that takes nothing away from Darwin's achievement. The idea now seems straightforward: "There is a struggle for existence leading to the preservation of profitable deviations of structure or instinct." Old species that could not adapt to changing climate or other conditions died out. New species that were adaptive reproduced themselves. The mechanism, natural selection, was based on random mutations, though Darwin did not know exactly how these occurred. He knew that there was variation within species. He knew that there must have been differential reproduction, because the fossil record showed that some species had died out. He knew that traits, adaptive and not so adaptive, were inherited. It was not until the middle of the next century that biologists, fully understanding the genetic basis of species' characteristics, pulled all the pieces of evolution together.[12]

Darwin was a cautious man and an even more circumspect biologist. As David Quammen has written in *The Reluctant Mr. Darwin*, "He never assembled a creed of scientific axioms and chiseled them on to a stone tablet beneath his own name. He was a reclusive biologist who wrote books. Sometimes he made mistakes. Sometimes he changed his mind." Darwin had hesitated to publish because he saw holes in his account. That is, he was worried that he had not gotten the science right. Because he could not experiment, he could not replicate results. In a fashion, the entire earth was his laboratory and all history of its living things his experiment. His method was to ask other researchers about their findings, to openly share his own concerns in correspondence and at meetings of scientific societies. He was willing to revise and republish. In short, he acted like a historian.[13]

The publication of Darwin's *The Origin of Species* caused a sensation. Biological scientists, geologists, men of the cloth, and educated readers all over the English-speaking world read it. "Everyone had an opinion. The book sold out of stores the first day; the country's largest circulating library made the *Origin* a selection; commuters read it on the train. Darwin's publisher rushed 3,000 more copies into print right away." From the moment he published he had scientific critics. "Some of Darwin's mentors

were shocked or scornful: astronomer John Herschel called natural selection 'the law of Higgledy piggledy.' But many younger men were full of
praise—biologist T. H. Huxley announced he was 'ready to go to the stake'
in Darwin's defense." St. George Mivart, a zoologist, believed that evolution
could not explain human consciousness. Wallace, whose own thinking on
evolution paralleled Darwin's, thought that environmental pressures rather
than competition among species was the key cause of evolution.[14]

Darwin extended his thinking to our own species in his *Descent of
Man* (1872).

Many of the views which have been advanced are highly speculative, and
some no doubt will prove erroneous; but I have in every case given the reasons which have led me to one view rather than to another. It seemed worth
while to try how far the principle of evolution would throw light on some of
the more complex problems in the natural history of man. . . . He who is not
content to look, like a savage, at the phenomena of nature as disconnected,
cannot any longer believe that man is the work of a separate act of creation.[15]

Evolution offers a model of historical change, a macrocosmic version
of history with human history as its most recent chapter, that dispenses
with religion altogether. Scientific findings replace Providence as the
prime mover. As the geneticist Richard Dawkins has written, "History
has been described as one damn thing after another . . . but this is an
impoverished view." Human history, like the grander story of the evolution of species, has patterns not imposed by human ingenuity so much
as by biological needs and opportunities. This is the "grand unifying
theory" of evolution writ small, of individuals and groups, peoples and
nations, that find in a harsh world ways to improve themselves and their
progeny. There is no place for a caring, immanent God in these theories.
The mechanisms of human history do not require divine assistance.[16]

Drawing the most extreme implications about religion and history
from Darwin's thought, scientists like Dawkins regard evolution as "the
ultimate consciousness-raiser" and dismiss religion as nonsense at best

and a murderous mistake at worst. To be sure, such judgments, clothed in historical examples, are not actually historical. Dawkins believes that the "Darwinian imperative" reveals, once and for all, that religion is a delusion. "Religion is so wasteful, so extravagant, and Darwinian selection habitually targets and eliminates waste." But atheism of the Dawkins sort is itself an ideology with a history, exponents, and critics, and no certain proof other than the ability to negate arguments for an immanent deity.[17]

Darwin was not conventionally religious himself, and his casual indifference to organized religion deeply concerned his wife, Emma; nevertheless, Darwin was aware that his idea would upset Christians. He was right. From the first, Darwin's ideas were not acceptable to some theologians on religious grounds. In 1873, the theologian and divinity school professor Charles Hodge devoted an entire book to refuting Darwin. What is Darwinism? he asked rhetorically. "It is atheism," for it was "utterly inconsistent with the Scriptures." The pope condemned the work, as did spokesmen for the Church of England. Some Christian critics were not quite so severe. Biologists like Louis Agassiz and Asa Gray, contemporaries of Darwin, proposed a compromise—God had permitted variation of the species, part of his ongoing involvement in the world. Thus evolution could be theistic. By the beginning of the twentieth century, liberal Christian leaders, particularly those in the van of progressive education, decried the equation of belief in evolution and atheism. As Wake Forest University President William Louis Poteat told an audience at the University of North Carolina in Chapel Hill, "fundamentalists 'were making it difficult for intelligent, educated men to be Christians.'"[18]

Natural selection might (and in time was) acceptable to many religious groups, but not to fundamentalists. They regarded the Bible story as divine truth, which meant that evolution could never be more than a theory. It could not be squared with the literal account of creation in the Bible, because God had created all the species at one time. In this version, the earth is young, not billions or even millions of years old, and creation occurred in seven days. Evolution requires the belief in epochs of supposed time and chance improvements. More sophisticated versions of religious-based criticism of evolution have modified creationism to argue that evolution is still a theory because it cannot be replicated in a laboratory. "The theory of intelligent design holds that certain features of the universe and of living things are best explained by an intelligent cause, not an undirected process such as natural selection." The intelligent design alternative to evolution is that over the course of geological time species have died out and new species have appeared but that the hand of God, not natural selection or any of its variants, controls the process. The divide between biological science, in particular the most respected and reputable teachers and researchers in the field, and the advocates of creationism and intelligent design is now unbridgeable.[19]

With most historians accepting some version of evolution, can one build a bridge between faith-inspired history and history that rejects such faith? The task seems difficult. To be sure, one can have faith in some superhuman force without belonging to any particular religious sect, but if history is the showcase of God's judgment of man, either the deepest springs of action are impenetrable to the scholar (who can truly know God's intent?) or one simply accepts that the flight of every sparrow is God's will. Either way, human agency has no efficacy. Ideals do not matter, including religious ideals, because the effective cause of all action is God, not man. At the same time, proposing that history means any one thing or another would simply be putting one's own words in God's mouth. To seek to know what cannot be known may be very human, but for fundamentalists of all stripes it is an affront to God's authority and a form of arrogant pride even in a pious person. In the Western tradition a religious person's passion for history is a passion for clues to individual and collective salvation—for one can seek evidence of one's own salvation even though one is utterly incapable of advancing it, not a quest for human meaning at all.

Seen in this admitted very narrow beam of light, the prospect of collaboration seemed doomed to fail. On the one hand, the great Christian religious chroniclers were not interested so much in explaining history as in defending faith. As Martin Cyril D'Arcy, a wise Jesuit philosopher and historian, conceded, "What seems to have happened is that the theologians took under their wing the subject of belief and thought and wrote about it as it interested them. This meant that they explored the Christian teaching of faith and were attracted to more general problems only in so far as they bore upon the nature of the supernatural act and habit." But the supernatural is precisely what historians cannot know, much less judge.[20]

On the other hand, with the apparent illogic of faith-based history so obvious to them, doggedly humanistic students of history scoffed at any and all attempts to provide a theological reading of the meaning of our past. As one of Voltaire's characters apologized, "Excuse the absurdity of my remarks. I have hitherto been a theologian, and one cannot divest oneself in a moment of every silly opinion." Twentieth-century secularist scholars were even harsher on a religious view of history. Arnold Toynbee's magisterial *A Study of History* illustrated and defended the retreat of the historians from anything resembling a providential interpretation of the past. Speaking of intolerance and religious violence, he wrote,

> This great blot upon our Western Civilization in the early modern age present . . . an extraordinary contrast to the rapid yet sure-footed contemporary progress of the same society in other directions; and the fact that religious intolerance, in this time and place, was not merely an absolute evil in itself, but was also a glaring anachronism[,] no doubt accounts in part for the unprecedented excesses to which it ran in the latest chapter of its history in the West.

Toynbee had his own explanation for the problem with religious accounts of historical events—organized religion itself was the source of evil. By the close of the twentieth century, the educated elite in the West were uncomfortable with religious insights into the meaning of the past. "Man's willingness to turn to history rather than to God for final judgment reveals how truly secular our culture and society have become. . . . In the process, the historian, whether he admits it or not, assumes the role of moral arbiter—a position traditionally accorded to the gods or the keepers of tradition. The judgment of history for a secular culture, therefore, can only mean the judgment of historians." The time when history was evidence to the educated layman of a providential will seems to have passed. The magister of American history in the second half of the twentieth century, Arthur M. Schlesinger Jr., in 1989 proposed that when it came to judgment of practical matters, "the American mind is by nature and tradition skeptical, irreverent, pluralistic and relativistic." Or was Schlesinger's obituary for religious history too hasty?[21]

"Non-Overlapping Magisteria"

A more sensitive intellectual tolerance than Schlesinger's might counsel students of history to travel a different path, a path along which spiritual values inspire the search for history's truths and scholarly canons direct that search to the realm of human action, desire, and thought. To adapt the zoologist Stephen J. Gould's remarkable little essay on religion and science, "[P]eople of goodwill wish to see [history] and religion at peace, working together to enrich . . . our lives." The way to achieve this objective is to regard history and religion as sovereign in separate realms. The first is a world of empirical facts—past human actions and expressions of thought and belief. The second is a world of faith and worship that cannot be proved or disproved according to accepted historical methods. Let a "respectful non-interference" be the principle upon which both realms operate. Gould called this arrangement "non-overlapping magisteria." For example, miraculous interpretations of human events would belong to religion, not history.[22]

A good scientist, Gould offered what seemed to him neutral rules to keep the two houses in order. To paraphrase them, first, the facts of history "are what they are, and cannot, in principle, resolve religious questions," except questions about the history of religion. Second, historians "remain free" to search for human meaning in human events, whatever the historians' religious beliefs might be, if any. Third, history is "amoral," to be written, judged, and applied "without reference to this strictly human concept" or morality. In this scheme, historical knowledge and religious faith would no longer be wary of each other, like feral cats eying one another as they mark the boundaries of their respective territories.[23]

A caveat: In this formulation, religious faith should not pit the historian's view of history against the ordinary person's—though that is what happens most often. In the so-called culture wars at the end of the twentieth century, local and state school boards were captured by born-again Protestants who had an agenda for the adoption of textbooks. According to Russell Shorto, "The one thing that underlies the entire program of the nation's Christian conservative activists is, naturally, religion. But it isn't merely the case that their Christian orientation shapes their opinions on gay marriage, abortion and government spending. More elementally, they hold that the United States was founded by devout Christians and according to biblical precepts." By contrast, good history can never be the tool of self-interested sectarianism.[24]

For much as one traditional Western religious historian might read and regard Scripture as holy, in the sense of its having been divinely inspired, history places the scripture—the writing—within the human rather than the divine time and place of its creation. As Garry Wills—a historian, a person of faith, and an interpreter of Scripture—has admonished readers, "To present ignorance of the history as a mystery to be revered is an exercise in false religiosity." His own view of the gospels, for example, concedes that "they are not historically true as that term would be understood today. They are not history at all, as our history is practiced." Their truth is of a different order and sort.[25]

✳   ✳   ✳

A religious sensibility could remind a historian of the frailties of the human heart and the limitations of the human intellect, though one need not be religious in any conventional sense of the word, or have faith in anything beyond the purview of science, to understand human frailties and limitations. In their later years, two American Marxian historians traveled this path. Both were critics of modernity, particularly mass production of ideas, uncritical faith in scientific progress, and cultural narcissism. Sometimes dismissed by their more liberal colleagues as neoconservatives or apostates from radicalism, they found in a religious sensibility a way to read the past. The first, Christopher Lasch, remained a skeptic. The second, Eugene Genovese, returned to his roots in Roman Catholicism. Neither concluded that history was God's Providence writ small, but both saw a limit to the claims that historians might make about their own work rooted deeply, if not overtly, in religious submission to a greater power.

A religious sensibility could tutor the scholar that everyone in the human family has feelings, aspirations, and needs, though an empathetic observer need not be a religious one. As Lasch wrote late in his life, "[T]he dangers of unlimited economic growth, unlimited technological development, unlimited exploitation of nature" should tutor every student of the past that there are limits, "a reminder both of our fallen state and our surprising capacity for gratitude, remorse, and forgiveness." Genovese put the case even more strongly: "Individualism . . . tends to place the state in hostile relation to society's discrete units, individual and corporate. Herein lies the principal germ of the dissolution of community itself." A purely rational academic discipline, like a purely rational society, becomes a raucous anarchy of ideas. Only through a faith in some unifying theme in common human aspiration can any humanistic study succeed. Historians need faith.[26]

Certainly, a tolerant study of history cannot tell us which faith is right, what is noble in our soul, or what we want from religion. A history whose religious impulse was "facile" or "self-indulgent" would not be good history. A history into which we pour our own beliefs, reading backward, is not good history. Instead, as Diarmaid MacCulloch writes in his sweeping history of Christianity, historians of religion and religious-minded historians "should seek to promote sanity and to curb the rhetoric which breeds fanaticism."[27]

For, in this sense, Western religion's foundational assertion that we are somehow created in a divine image underlay the Western historical enterprise. Without the assumption of a basic similarity among people then and now, a kind of universal human nature, no scholar could begin to seek insight into the motives of people who lived long ago. This sort of sensibility, historically rooted in a Judeo-Christian assumption about the divine, elevated the historian, allowing him or her to stand as "judge and arbiter, counsel and witness." Like the Almighty on the holiest of days, "you write and you seal, you record and recount. You remember deeds long forgotten." Once, long ago, religious sensibility empowered the historical vision and gave depth and meaning to historical judgments. It is a debt historians should honor.[28]

[2]

History and Philosophy

History is philosophy teaching by examples.

DIONYSIUS OF HALICARNASSUS,
Ars Rhetorica (first century B.C.E.)

Like religion and history, philosophy and history have a long, complicated, sometimes fruitful and sometimes difficult relationship. Perhaps the awkwardness in the collaboration is a byproduct of professional instincts. Historians are wary of addressing basic questions of knowing. Philosophers revel in those same questions. But questions of how we know about the past and how we present that knowledge are not just matters of historical method. They run deeper, as an examination of the ties between history and philosophy reveals. David Hume said it even better, in part because he was a superb philosopher as well as a meticulous chronicler, "the most historically minded of philosophers and the most subtly and profoundly philosophical of historians." Writing of the morality of obedience to tyrants in his *Treatise of Human Nature*, Hume coupled the two disciplines: "For there is a principle of human nature, which we have frequently taken notice of, that men are mightily addicted to general rules, and that we often carry our maxims beyond those reasons, which first induc'd us to establish them. Where cases are similar in many circumstances, we are apt to put them on the same footing, without considering that they differ in the most material circumstances, and that the resemblance is more apparent than real." The real test of the reliability of any statement of fact was reference to its history. "To give an instance of this, we may chuse any point of history, and consider for what reason we either believe or reject it."[1]

With Hume's injunctions in mind—and read correctly as joining rather than uncoupling history and philosophy—one can and should ask if history is really philosophy teaching by example. Can the writing of history incorporate the moral concerns of the philosophers, or is historical scholarship inherently amoral? Are ideas timeless like the shadows on Plato's cave, or are they merely products of a place and time? In the final analysis, historians and philosophers must talk to each other in an ongoing collaborative endeavor.[2]

The prime obstacle to a fruitful conversation between historians and philosophers is jargon. For example, the *Companion* to the philosophy of history divides the field into the philosophy of history proper and the philosophy of historiography. The former is a branch of philosophy. The latter is the study of all beliefs, values, and ideas in the past. I take this to be simply intellectual history with a hard shell of jargon. Even the editor of the *Companion* finds this "a distinction that does not exist in any natural language or philosophical jargon" (and subsequent distinctions of its kind) "too vague" to be useful. I have to second that motion—I had no idea what the distinctions distinguished.[3]

With all due respect to the differences between the following approach and the way in which working philosophers might approach this same subject, I think that four overlapping concerns of philosophers and historians impose vital connections between the ways in which the two disciplines operate: what is the source of morality, what is the authority of reason and reasoned argument, what is the nature of causation, and what are ideas. When one explores these, one sees how intertwined history and philosophy are and must be.

Morality

From the inception of historical writing, some historians and philosophers have assumed that history illustrated principles of morality and true philosophy reveals itself in historical studies. They concluded that history, by an unerring and persistent search for truth, was essential to the philosopher. It was the working out in human time and space of essential rational truths. In turn, the philosophical method—dispassionate, objective, deeply in touch with the laws of nature—appealed to early modern historians. As the English historian and antiquarian Richard Braithwaite wrote in 1638, "[T]he true use and scope of all histories ought to tend to no other purpose, than . . . to caution us in things offensive, and incite us to the management of imployments in themselves generous, and worthy of imitation." George Bancroft, the widely read and greatly admired Democratic historian of the United States, thought doing history was a moral enterprise. As he wrote in 1834, at the beginning of his multi-volume history of the United States, "[P]opular freedom rests on the sanctity of morals." The most cogent recent argument for the moral imperative in history belongs to David Harlan. He boldly stated that the purpose of historical study is to "force us to ponder what might lie behind our own best wishes and good intentions." History allows its students to "respect the dead" only by allowing them "to speak to the living."[4]

Many early modern philosophers of history found the two disciplines tied together by common concern for moral principles. In the first part of the nineteenth century, the German thinker Georg Hegel went so far as to build a philosophy of history in which moral principle was the determining force behind all historical action. Hegel explored the implications of this philosophy of history in his university lectures. Great events were not accidents, and history was not a collection of foolish happenings. Chance affected all human activity, of this there could be no denial, but the Spirit that appeared everywhere in history took larger steps toward its goal of Reason. The process was the now-famous dialectic, in which great movements gave rise to their antitheses, until a synthesis, the manifestation of Reason, allowed people to advance to a new stage of self-awareness.[5]

Hegel offered a resolution to the apparent disjoint among the historian's love of facts, the particularity of human action and thought, and the philosopher's adherence to general principles applicable to a wide variety of historical events:

It is the aim of the investigator to gain a view of the entire history of a people or a country, or of the world, in short, what we call Universal History. In this case the working up of the historical material is the main point. The workman approaches his task with his own spirit; a spirit distinct from that of the element he is to manipulate. Here a very important consideration will be the principles to which the author refers, the bearing and motives of the actions and events which he describes, and those which determine the form of his narrative.

Philosophical detachment enabled the objective historians to see the big picture. Hegel cautioned scholars wedded to more narrow-gauge approaches, "A history which aspires to traverse long periods of time, or to be universal, must indeed forgo the attempt to give individual representations of the past as it actually existed. It must foreshorten its pictures by abstractions; and this includes not merely the omission of events and deeds, but whatever is involved in the fact that Thought is, after all, the most trenchant epitomist." The lesson: History and philosophy were twinned because the moral principles in the latter controlled what happened in the former. Too much historical detail only clouded the historian's visions of philosophical truths.[6]

Hegel's approach was attractive to Karl Marx, as he formulated his own philosophical history. Hegel's philosophy of history merely framed the principle of Reason. Marx filled in the canvas with political and economic detail. Although I prefer to treat Marx in this chapter as a moral philosopher who used history, one might almost as easily include him in the chapter on the social sciences and history, so pervasively influential were his contributions to those fields.

Marx was born in Prussia and married into the gentry there, but he found Germany unreceptive to his increasingly radical political ideas and migrated to France, Belgium, and finally England with his longtime collaborator and sometime patron Friedrich Engels. Marx and Engels burst onto the philosophical scene with the *Communist Manifesto* (1848). Their plan for economic reform incorporated elements of current socialist thought but went far beyond these to argue for a classless state in which all men and women would be equal in law and wealth. In his later, more complex writings on history and philosophy, Marx borrowed the dialectic notion of historical change, though he objected to Hegel's emphasis on the progress of thought. Marx was a materialist, not an idealist. History was not the becoming of the idea of Reason as Hegel forecast but a struggle for control of the means of production that passed through several set stages. The last of these stages, true equality of possession and production through communism, was the destined end of history.[7]

Like Hegel's, Marx's philosophy of history reached deeply into moral concerns. It may indeed "be pointless to search for a single theory of history" in his work, but there can be no doubt that for him history had deep structures that inevitably dictated its course, and these were fundamentally moral. The base of all history was labor and capital, the ongoing struggle of worker and owner. All the ideas, the culture and the religion, that one could find were but a superstructure built upon that foundation. "In changing the modes of production, mankind changes all its social relations. The hand mill creates a society with the feudal lord; the steam mill a society with the industrial capitalist. . . . Under the patriarchal system, under the caste system, under the feudal and corporative system, there was division of labor in the whole of society according to fixed rules." In the end, the struggle could lead only to the ideal moral state of men—a state wherein each gave to others and those in need were never needy. It was a utopian idea of a classless state based on a genuine sharing of material goods.[8]

Most modern historians and philosophers are chary of such overarching theories, particularly those linking historical reasons to philosophical Reason. "Most historians . . . would dismiss all such attempts to describe the process of change as failures." But the dream of a perfect history resting upon a perfect philosophy still tantalizes us in the moments between sleep and wakefulness.[9]

When there were philosophical voices raised against any overly neat conjunction of moral philosophy and historical dialectic, they sounded not in the rejection of a philosophical history but in an alternative version of moral theory for history. For these critics, history simply taught a more complicated moral lesson than either Hegel or Marx provided. At the end of the nineteenth century, a century replete with historians speaking with the greatest certitude about the deep philosophical principles of history and philosophers finding in history proofs of eternal verities, Friedrich Nietzsche rejected these connections in a way that continues to challenge everyone concerned with the interplay of philosophy and history.

As a young man, Nietzsche was an academic of immense promise. He was appointed to a chair in classical philology at 24, and ten years later ill health forced his resignation and the end of his teaching career. His philosophical essays did not sell well. He lamented, after the publication of *Beyond Good and Evil* in 1886, that of the 300 in print, his publisher had sold only 114 copies. Perhaps one problem was his literary style. His philosophical essays, commencing in 1878, were organized in aphorisms, short bursts of genius punctuated by splenetic outbursts of despair. Though infections contracted during his service in the German army (he was a medical orderly) would eventually lead to his physical and mental collapse, the uniqueness of his criticism and philosophy grew in proportion to his withdrawal from everyday affairs. A virtual recluse in his later years, he was loved, admired, hated, and denounced. No one doubted, however, that his was one of the greatest minds of his age, "still talked about and written about."[10]

The nineteenth-century philosophers and historians agreed that evil, want, and suffering would soon be forgotten. Nietzsche demurred from that facile conclusion. While the standard of living (life expectancy, literacy, the quality of food, housing, and clothing) had improved for the common man, nothing had changed about the way in which men and women viewed their world. Philosophers and historians who catered to the vulgar masses only obscured the fundamental problem. "Books for all the world are always foul-smelling books: the smell of small people clings to them."[11]

Though he was not known as a philosopher of history, Nietzsche's notions of history played a key part in his larger assault on conventional ideas. History proved to him that "man veils and subdues the past," by which he meant that historians had failed in their duty to see the world as he did. "There could be a kind of historical writing that had no drop of common fact in it and yet could claim to be called in the highest degree objective." Instead, he judged all history to be subjective, a product of individual need and bias. He did not have much use for the university-trained historical scholars of his day either, seeing them as neither masculine nor feminine but as "mere neuters" looking for truth in all the wrong places.[12]

Nietzsche found in history a kind of ur-morality. History taught what conventional philosophy denied, that "placing one's will on a par with that of someone else," the golden rule at the core of Christian morality, was "really . . . a will to the denial of life, a principle of disintegration and decay." Equality of treatment among natural equals was healthy, but not among unequals. Such "sentimental weakness" ignored the fact, proven in history, that all life "simply is the will to power." The master's morality would and should never bow to the slave's morality. "Therefore it is a gross mistake when historians of morality" ignore the instinctual differences of a noble spirit and a subservient one.[13]

For Nietzsche, history taught that there were no great ideas. There were only great men. Their nobility of spirit, manifested in part by their challenge to convention, was all that history or philosophy could offer to later generations. This guiding principle led him to oppose democratic reforms and egalitarian laws. They denied, in his view, what nature demanded— rule by the superior beings. Perhaps his conclusion was inevitable from his first premise: There was no objective truth, no Reason or law, no God, nothing that ordained fair play, love of the other, self-sacrifice for the good of the whole, or anything like these false ideals. But in the end Nietzsche did not divorce history from morality. He merely substituted the morality of the superman for the conventional morality of his day. Nihilism had its own morality, rooted in what he took to be historical fact.[14]

Nietzsche did not have the last word, though his moral nihilism seemed appropriate to the madness of Nazism, a philosophy of history that drew its inspiration in part from his works. In opposition to that facile wedding

of superman amorality and nationalism, many humane, liberal philosophers raised objections. The most compelling of these voices was Karl
Popper's. Popper was a secular Viennese Jew and one of the twentieth
century's foremost philosophers. He had lived through history in its raw-
est form—the German program to erase European Jewry, including the
intellectual contributions of Jews to European life. Yet he clung to the idea
that liberal democracy and scientific inquiry could still save the world
from tyrants and their madness. For him, it was the effort of solving problems that makes us human, not absolute knowledge. So he rejected what
he called historicism, "the theory that society will necessarily change but
along a predetermined path that cannot change, through stages predetermined by inexorable necessity." Instead, "There is no logical path" leading
to objective and universal truths. "They can only be reached by intuition,
based upon something like an intellectual love of the objects of experience." The judgment of the historian was rooted in the morality of a liberal
conscience. One might even say that Popper rescued the philosophy of
history from history—that is, he reminded the philosophical community
that history could teach valuable moral lessons, even though the forces of
absolutist tyranny would bend historical accounts to their own uses. As he
wrote in *The Open Society and Its Enemies*, "We can interpret the history
of power politics from the point of view of our fight for the open society,
for a rule of reason, for justice, freedom, equality, and for the control of
international crime" like Nazism and Stalinism.[15]

A historian reading the foregoing paragraphs on Nietzsche's heroic
anarchism and Popper's ordered liberty will remark that the two thinkers'
philosophies of history were responses to their own experience and the
larger intellectual currents of their times. (A philosopher reading the same
lines will say, quite rightly, that five pages cannot begin to describe the
complexities of the two philosophers' ideas.) My point is that moral ideas
and their formulations may seem universal to philosophers or schools of
philosophy, but the historians will see how moral philosophies and their
expositors go in and out of fashion. It is a mistake to read the philosopher

as a fellow philosopher would, for this would de-contextualize philosophical writings. As the historian Charles Beard explained to a 1933 meeting of the American Historical Association, "The philosopher, possessing little or no acquaintance with history, sometimes pretends to expound the inner secret of history, but the historian turns upon him and expounds the secret of the philosopher, as far as it may be expounded at all, by placing him in relation to the movement of ideas and interests in which he stands or floats, by giving to his scheme of thought its appropriate relativity."

Proof of this critique lies in the way in which later generations read Nietzsche and Popper, readings shaped by changed contexts. Instead of indelible words and universally applicable ideas, their contributions are read in the light of contemporary events. Nietzsche, for example, was welcomed in the America of H. L. Mencken as the ultimate individualist, reviled during World War II as the forerunner of soulless totalitarianism, resurrected in the 1950s as a defender of human choice, and criticized in the 1970s as the first of the postmodern relativists. Nietzsche, who believed he was an original and rejected slavish imitations, became whatever the historical moment claimed of him. He became a palette on which readers could paint their own "moral outlooks." Popper, once lionized for his liberal views, has faced similar revisionism. Martin Gardiner, perhaps the most respected popular writer on science and mathematics in the second half of the twentieth century, concluded, "Today [Popper's] followers among philosophers of science are a diminishing minority, convinced that Popper's vast reputation is enormously inflated. I agree. I believe that Popper's reputation was based mainly on this persistent but misguided effort to restate common-sense views in a novel language that is rapidly becoming out of fashion."[16]

Although historians may prove that the reputations and the particular ideas of individual philosophers are creatures of time and place—that is, of history itself—when historians themselves write, their language always has some larger moral tenor. Historians cannot escape such judgment in their writing. Consider this example: If the historian introduces George Washington's march to the forks of the Ohio in 1754 as a "daring and resourceful twenty-one-year-old messenger sent on a dangerous mission into the American wilderness," the reader will regard the event and the man as heroic. Had the historian chosen other words, the reader would regard Washington's introduction to war differently, as in this recounting: Young Washington has just witnessed his Indian allies killing wounded French soldiers: "By afternoon, Washington was back at his own camp, groping for explanations and trying to plan his next move. Since boyhood he had dreamed of battle's glory. Now he had seen combat but no heroism: only chaos and the slaughter of defenseless men." The moral sentiments aroused by the two accounts are not a matter of difference of opinion among historians that a greater attention to the primary source evidence could resolve. All depictive language judges. As the philosopher Peter Winch has written, "[A]ny worthwhile study of society must be philosophical in character and any worthwhile philosophy must be concerned with the nature of human society." Judging ideas in history must be infused with moral philosophy. History teaches that notions of good and evil are contextual. "The idea gets its sense from the role it plays in the system. . . . The relation between idea and context is an internal one." The connection lies in the words used to describe good and evil in the past and in the present. "To give an account of the meaning of a word is to describe how it is used; and to describe how it is used is to describe the social intercourse into which it enters." The historian, tied to the words in his or her primary sources, becomes something like the simultaneous interpreter at the United Nations, turning past moral expressions—the ideals of a people—into modern language.[17]

The modern historian may protest that any moralizing in historical scholarship, whether part of a larger project of a philosophical history or more closely tied to particular events and people, must be excised from historians' writings. In his list of "historians' fallacies," the historian David Hackett Fischer conceded that moral judgment was not the same as moralizing, for the historian cannot keep "value assumptions" out of his or her work but can avoid the moralistic fallacy: moral opinion masquerading as historical fact. Is Fischer guilty of his own fallacy—condemning the immorality of a profession unaware of its moral obligation not to make moral judgments? In any case, labeling something as a fallacy does not mean it can be excised without losing a vital part of history.[18]

Consider Gordon Wright's magnificent presidential address at the American Historical Association meeting in 1975. "The idea of consciously reintroducing the moral dimension into history runs counter to the basic training of most historians, and probably to their professional instinct as well. Each of us has some strong views on the general subject of morality; each of us knows the dangers involved in making moral judgments in our work, or even suggesting a need for them." But the Vietnam War had influenced an entire generation of historians, many of them sitting in the ballroom in Atlanta to hear Wright, and he continued, "Neither our audience nor the condition of the world in which we live any longer allows us the luxury of escape into a Proustian cork-lined ivory tower free of dust, microbes, and values. . . . No doubt those of us who profess contemporary history have found the dilemma sharpest; whoever must deal with the more brutal aspects of the Hitler or Stalin era, or with the devastating mass impact of mechanized total war, finds it hard to restrain some expression of that righteous indignation." If history is to mean anything to its audience, it must recognize that moral judgment is embedded in historians' accounts. For Stanley Fish, bringing such concerns explicitly into scholarship is inherently to bias one's findings, bending fact around the desired results. Nothing the historian does, as a teacher or scholar, can foster moral character. But as Jane Kamensky asked, "Does exploring aspects of the past that coincide with urgent matters of present-day concern cheapen or deepen historical writing?" The historian has a potent weapon in his or her findings, and the dramatic depiction of those findings, in the battle for social justice.[19]

In the end, the historian's moral judgments remain those of his or her time. But history can lead the mind "from the calm closets of philosophical inquirers, where they have delighted and elevated the minds of the few, into the world of life and action" where moral judgment and ideas are never abstract formulations.[20]

Reason

As the brief discussion of Hegel suggested, the notion of Reason and the ideal of reasoned argument are common to both history and philosophy. A faith in the authority of reason is rooted in Western culture, going as far back in time as the Socratic dialogues (and probably earlier, for fortune has seen fit to preserve only a tiny fraction of classical Greek philosophers' writings). For Socrates and his alter ego Plato, even the elusive mysteries of the soul could be revealed only by reason. As Socrates tells Glaucon about the soul at the end of *The Republic*: "Her immortality is demonstrated by the previous argument, and there are many other proofs; but to see her as she really is, not as we now behold her, marred by communion with the body and other miseries, you must contemplate her with the eye of reason."[21]

Reason spoke directly to Socrates, but not to his fellow Athenians. The more he harangued his countrymen about politics, law, and war, the angrier they became. When he was tried for treason, he impudently told them that reason dictated they acquit him. When he was convicted and asked to leave the city, reason directed suicide instead. Uncompromising ratiocination led to unmerited death. Had Socrates perhaps failed to understand that the ideal of a reasoned life is not the same as a life of logic chopping? Logic is a closed mathematical system enabling us to prove the validity of certain conclusions based on certain propositions. If the propositions are false, no amount of logical argument can make them true.[22]

Nor should historians conflate reason with motive. Historians deal with motive all the time, putting themselves in the place of their subjects and asking, were they X, knowing what X knew then, having the same ambitions as X, how they would have acted. When historians do this, they are reasoning as X might have reasoned. This "rationality principle" is the way in which historians make sense of individual decisions, but how can they be sure that they have X's reasoning right? Human rationality is not a universal element of history, like the forms in the *Republic*. Instead, reason is a cultural construction, a byproduct of human desire and literacy in given times and places. In other words, no law of nature dictates the outcome of any human reasoning. The historian's learned intuition cannot claim any more than the chance of being correct.[23]

Could the historian nevertheless join formal logic and learned intuition to reach historical truths? The historian who believes in some form of "covering law" will argue that correct results can be deduced from a sufficiency of factual evidence: Simply find the category in which the events fit and apply the right law to deduce what really happened. The empiricist will argue the opposite, inducting or inferring truth from the consonance of past and present. The empiricist need not categorize it but will know it when he or she sees it. But here's the rub: The deductive historian and the empirical historian face the same obstacle. Both must choose words to describe things. The choice is neither arbitrary nor dictated by any law of logic. When is a patriot a rebel? When is a terrorist a freedom fighter? On the eve of the American Revolution, the rebels (or patriots) called the loyalists "Tories" and referred to themselves as "Whigs." These terms came into use at the end of the seventeenth century in England. A Tory was a defender of the absolute power of kings, according to the Whigs; and a Whig was a rebel, according to the Tories. When historians choose among these terms to describe the opposing sides in 1775, they are joining in the debate rather than standing above it. To repeat, historians know that words in statements they make, just like the statements made by people in the past, depend for their meaning not on the logic of the statement itself but on meanings that real people in real time ascribe to the words.[24]

Nor are historians above the mischance of logical fallacy, misusing the rules of argument, either intentionally or by accident. In 1970, David Hackett Fischer's *Historians' Fallacies* presented a relentless and somewhat humorless exposé of the illogical arguments famous historians made. Fischer worried that "[t]he work of too many professional historians is diminished by an antirational obsession—by an intense prejudice against method, logic, and science. . . . [I]n fact historians . . . go blundering about their business without a sufficient sense of purpose or procedure." Fischer regarded all fallacies as "wrong turnings." They misled; they misrepresented; they were wrong. Avoiding them, his challenge to us, would make historical scholarship—and the lessons of history—more trustworthy. But Fischer's remarkable catalogue of slips and slides into fallacy by the foremost historians never explained why such fine scholars were guilty of such elementary mistakes.[25]

The answer is "necessity." Historical writing is not an exercise in logical argument so much as an exercise in creative imagination. Historians try to do the impossible: retrieve an ever-receding and thus never reachable past. Given that the task is impossible, one cannot be surprised that historians must occasionally use fallacy—hasty generalization, weak analogy, counterfactual hypotheticals, incomplete comparisons, and even jumping around in past time and space to glimpse the otherwise invisible yesteryear. All the historian can ask of the philosopher here is tolerance, and all the philosopher can require of the historian is honesty about the methods used.

Causation

A third tie between the two disciplines revolves around the question of causation. Aristotle taught that causation is an essential part of knowledge. We cannot fully comprehend anything until we know why it happened. Two of his four types of causation concern the historian: the "efficient cause" (the immediate forces impelling change) and "final cause" (the purpose for which the change occurred). None of Aristotle's metaphysics really helps the historian directly, for both types of causes seem either obvious or impenetrable. Either the historian asserted that X caused Y or the historian conceded that we could never know the precise cause of Y. For cause was nothing more than the events preceding those under study.[26]

David Hume pooh-pooh'd such metaphysical inquiries into causation as Aristotle's when he announced that cause was not a solid thing like a link in a chain but simply the constant conjunction of sets of events in our minds. "If all the long chain of causes and effects, which connect any past event with any volume of history, were compos'd of parts different from each other, and which 'twere necessary for the mind distinctly to conceive, 'tis impossible we shou'd preserve to the end any belief or evidence. But as most of these proofs are perfectly resembling, the mind runs easily along them, jumps from one part to another with facility, and forms but a confus'd and general notion of each link." Experience, not some law of nature, put these conjunctions where we could see them. Imputing to them some deeper, autonomous, automatic mechanism was just philosophical mischief. Hume was also a historian, so his rejection of mechanical theories of causation seemed then, and still seems, to make a lot of sense.[27]

But philosophical inquiries into the nature of causation by historians were not going to satisfy the philosophers. In fact, the reverse seems to be the case. Hume's casual empiricism seemed to throw down the gauntlet to later academic philosophers of history. At least Immanuel Kant said that Hume's skepticism had woken him from his slumbers. The result was Kant's fervent belief that history was properly viewed only from a philosophical perspective. In his essay "Ideas for a Universal History from a Cosmopolitan Point of View" (1784), Kant engaged in a circular argument—that history revealed laws of nature and laws of nature governed history—but no matter; the essence was that historical causes were not, as Hume believed, simple products of human intellection. Causes and effects could be predicted in general.[28]

In the twentieth century, the most important philosophical attempt to revisit Hume's commonsense historical empiricism was Karl Hempel's. Hempel was a German logician and philosopher of science who migrated to the United States in 1939 and thereafter held a number of university positions of increasing repute. He was best known for arguing that scientific laws were not trustworthy as predictions of the future. They were instead reliable descriptions of what was happening in the here and now. In 1942, Hempel expressed his theory of "covering laws" of history in terms of formal logic. In a world at war, a formal logic of historical law seemed about as comforting a philosophy of history as one could get, though Hempel and his followers would surely reject such an empirical explanation of their endeavor. In any case, the theory went like this: Assume that general laws exist. If, then, a series of causes—say, C_1, C_2, C_3, and so on—always came before an event, it could be said that there was a general law covering the causation of that event. Setting aside the initial assumption of covering laws (isn't that what we need to prove?), if this formulation is to be something more than a tautology, one must know a great deal more about the causes of events than we know (or can know). After all, any event of any significance is always preceded by an infinity of prior events. Which of them are relevant (even assuming we could know them all) and which too far off to have any effect on the event is a matter of historical interpretation.[29]

Now the inquiry gets complicated. For Hempel, historical interpretation had two meanings. The first is the interpretation of the veracity, utility, and meaning of specific pieces of historical evidence. The second is the interpretation of a historical event. The latter requires placing the event in the most relevant of the many historical contexts in which every event existed. That context (where one is bidden to look for the covering law) can be quite narrow or very broad.[30]

For example, on the third day of the Gettysburg battle, General Robert E. Lee decided upon a massive frontal attack on Union positions on Cemetery Ridge. He ordered three divisions of infantry to attack abreast. The event, celebrated in Civil War history as Pickett's Charge, was the "high water mark" of the Confederacy's military effort in the eastern theater, and the result was the near-destruction of a third of Lee's Army of Northern Virginia. What caused him to make this decision? Was it frustration at the lack of progress during the previous two days? Was it the sense that a desperate gamble to break through the Army of the Potomac and march on Washington, D.C., was the only way to end the war? Was Lee, ill with dysentery, simply losing his customary mastery of tactics? Were there no other options? (Lee's chief subordinate, General James Longstreet, advised a march around the left flank of the Union forces instead of a frontal attack.) Because these questions resist answers, we have to think of Lee's decision, and the events that followed, in a broader context. Gettysburg was one battle in the many fought over the bloody ground between Richmond, Virginia, and Washington, D.C. One must factor into the equation the state of the opposing forces over the first three years of war, the theories of war that both sides carried with them from the Mexican-American War to the Civil War, and the state of politics in the Union and Confederacy. All these and more considerations broaden the context. Should we also consider concepts of honor and loyalty, of manliness and idealism, the antebellum young men bore into the fight?

Even assuming the covering law into which these sequences of facts fit exists, the historian knows that no covering law, no general laws, can completely comprehend either the efficient or the final causation of what happened on July 3, 1863, at Gettysburg. But every historian knows that each decision made that day, and the day before, and the day before that, and in the weeks following the Confederate victory at Chancellorsville in May, contributed to the outcome of Pickett's Charge. Philosophical discourses on the nature of causation are no help here, but philosophical rigor in thinking about causation is.

As explanations for the coming of a major event—the Civil War, for example—philosophical notions of causation teach the historian that when a series of small causal events seems inadequate as an explanation, the historian must raise the level of generality of his or her explanation. In this sense, Hempel was on the right track. Bleeding Kansas (1854–60), divisive Supreme Court decisions like *Dred Scott v. Sanford* (1857), and even the victory of the Republican Party at the polls in 1860 did not cause the Civil War, because the divisiveness of very similar events in previous years were muted by compromises. Secession rested not on politics but on precisely what Lincoln said in his 1858 debates with Stephen A. Douglas: "A house divided against itself" over slavery could not stand. Without a nation that was half slave and half free, there would have been no Civil War. Thus an explanation can be found at a higher level of generality. Call this a covering law and Hempel smiles down upon us.

Ideas

A final issue of common concern may make collaborators of historians and philosophers in a more substantial way than shared moralism, reasoned argument, and causation: the pursuit of the meaning of ideas. The noble dream of a philosophical history in which the historian is the judge "before which men and nations pass in review" is a "truly philosophical history." It "expresses simply the normative urge of reason and conscience seeking some power of total vision above the heat of strife." It is a dream that requires one small assumption (typically of logic—one begins not with realities but with assumptions about reality), that "unless the genuineness of values, transcendence, and constant relations is granted, knowledge is impossible." In other words, values cannot be so relative to time and place that the scholar in another time and place cannot imagine what ideas were like then and there. This is called idealist history. To understand how it ties history and philosophy, we need to examine its close cousin, the "history of ideas."[31]

Ideas are as slippery as eels and as powerful as the sun. They explain, motivate, attract, and repel. They are essential to civilized life, for they are the containers of human wisdom, know-how, and belief from generation to generation and era to era. When we write history about ideas in history we give the idea a permanent public form. At the same time, we interpret the meaning of past thoughts. We analyze, asking and answering where ideas originated, how they changed, and what impact they had upon action.

Some ideas are great—that is, they have great influence on the course of history. Some ideas are also ideals, like democracy and equality. Some ideas are hateful to us, like racism and "ethnic cleansing" (though others in different times and places have embraced those ideas). However the professional historian or the consumer of history feels about any particular idea, when we read about the history of ideas or hear about it in lectures, ideas are passed on to us. How else would we know that the idea of greatness appears in one form or another in every culture and in every time period, at least those for which written or oral evidence survives? As flimsy and controversial as they may be, ideas have a staying power that transcends time and place.

But what is an idea, that anyone can know and judge it? It may be that for all humans, certain ideas are hardwired into our mental apparatus. That, at least, is what two of the greatest thinkers of the twentieth century, the cultural anthropologist Claude Lévi-Strauss and the psychoanalyst Carl Jung, have made to our store of ideas. (Note that I take the license of treating the two thinkers as philosophers rather than as anthropologist and psychoanalyst, respectively. I do this because it is their philosophy of knowing that interests me, not the academic box in which they, or others, happened to put them.)

Lévi-Strauss's life spanned the twentieth century and in it he stood astride the field of cultural anthropology. Generalizing from his work with Brazilian Indians in the half-decade before the outbreak of World War II, he demolished the nineteenth-century distinction between the savage mind and the civilized mind, so vital to the rationale for European imperialism. During the first years of the war he served in the French Army, and after France capitulated and Germany occupied France, like other Jewish intellectuals (notably the historian Marc Bloch), Lévi-Strauss was denied employment and faced the imminent threat of deportation to the concentration camps. He was able to flee, ultimately to New York City, and there found a supportive circle of other émigrés from Nazi tyranny. He formed a strong bond with the American Jewish anthropologist Franz Boas, a friendship that broadened Lévi-Strauss's view of his discipline. Boas taught that "the antagonisms" which racial stereotypes fostered had no place in anthropology, that there was no "racial heredity" and that prejudice was "easily misled by general impressions." Written in 1928, at the height of the Jim Crow era, these were courageous words. They echoed in Lévi-Strauss's own essay "Race and History" (1950) for UNESCO. It had not escaped the attention of either man that Hitler and his cohort defined the Jews as a race. In 1942, Boas collapsed and died in Lévi-Strauss's arms.[32]

Returning to France in 1948, Lévi-Strauss soon gained his doctorate, published his studies, and was appointed to a chair at the College of France. His philosophy of cultural anthropology bid his readers see ideas in "structural" terms, as "basic similarities between forms of social life" governed by the "universal laws which make up the unconscious activity of the mind." Lévi-Strauss's search for commonalities, or structures, in myths extended to art, learning, religion, and all the other cultural expressions of a people, linking what seemed to be the distinct and individual to larger, shared ways of thinking. Such mental structures were supposed to be real; they lay beneath ways of thinking as disparate as sorcery and theology.[33]

The psychologist Carl Jung asserted the same notion of universal forms in his analysis of the ideas or archetypes in the collective unconscious mind. Born and educated in Switzerland at the end of the nineteenth century, Jung never faced the personal animosities and physical dangers that Lévi-Strauss encountered. Instead, his turmoil came from within, a spirit divided between middle-class modernity and something far more mystical. He developed phobias as a youngster, as well as fainting spells that his later studies in analytic psychology helped him tackle. His close association, followed by a falling out, with Sigmund Freud, and his lifelong wrestling match with religion (his father was a country pastor), also found their way into his thought.

Jung's contributions to psychiatry were as profound as Lévi-Strauss's to anthropology. These included the idea of introverted and extroverted personalities, the notion of a bundle of neuroses combining into a "complex," and the concept of the archetype. The archetype was a "nucleus of meaning" about which there circled a variety of images and feelings depending on the particular culture in which an individual was nurtured. For example, the mother goddess archetype "is often associated with things and places standing for fertility and fruitfulness, the cornucopia, a ploughed field, a garden." Hollow objects might also suggest the mother goddess. These might be positive or negative in their connotation. Along with the mother, the spirit, the trickster, and rebirth were found everywhere and everywhere had powerful influences upon culture.[34]

If the historian were to express skepticism of such impressionistically defined and globally applicable ideas, seeing both Lévi-Strauss's structuralism and Jung's archetypes as part of the history of anthropology and psychiatry respectively (see Charles Beard's address quoted above) rather than as part of a useful historical methodology, Lévi-Strauss and Jung nevertheless have a good deal to say to historians of ideas. In fact, what they say may be essential to the very project of doing the history of ideas. It seems to me that one must assume some kind of continuity, some connection, between the ideas of people in the past and the mind of the historian (and his or her reader) today, or intellectual history slides into the realm of historical fiction. Whenever the historian claims the ability to know and to be able to explain what people long ago meant and thought, the historian is relying on some kind of demonstrable continuity. In an even more basic way, if the historian of ideas can claim to understand what words written long ago meant, the historian must posit some kind of continuity. "We, as humans, make our world comprehensible by imposing mental structures upon it."[35]

To summarize: The historian claims to know past ideas with the same confidence with which the philosopher claims to know ideas in the here and now. But for a moment let us take now the other side of the case and assume the null hypothesis that such an idealist history, a history of ideas resting on the collaboration of history and philosophy, is not possible. To recapitulate: The null hypothesis would reject the notion of continuity between past and present as an unsustainable postulate. Following this logic, the only way to defend the continuity would be to show that historians in the present can understand past ideas, and that is the very presumption that the null hypothesis questions. The continuity would thus appear to be an example of a circular argument.[36]

But idealist history does not rest on logic. Its advocates insist that historical proof is not the same as scientific proof but is possible only because of the unique characteristics that people in the past and people like the historian share. If ideas are simply the product of personal experience, then no genuine empathy is possible without the historian's duplicating the experience of his or her subject. If such near-identities of experience were impossible, the entire project of empathy would fail.[37]

What can bridge the gap of years and context and make such idealist empathy work? The answer is the historian's imagination. For Wilhelm Dilthey, the German intellectual historian whose lectures on historical imagination are still staples of idealist history, the historical imagination is akin to the poetic imagination. According to Dilthey, the poet can be understood by later historians because and only insofar as the poetry has drawn upon "a basic trait of life." The historian of literature or art assesses the impact of his or her subject through imaginative association. The historical account of the poem or painting works because of the (admittedly presupposed) common aesthetics of imagination. The historian learns what the artist knew about his or her own work and uses that to fuel the historical imagination, figuratively taking the scholar back to the artist's time and place. Because "thoughts sustain themselves independently of their original context," the historian's imagination permits him or her to know the past. Perhaps even more important, as poetry or pictorial arts are true to themselves, so the art of the historical account may be true to itself, works of art like those it studies. By extension, all history is possible to the idealist historian.[38]

The idea that ideas floated in some ether apart from the human condition did not seem to fit the American intellectual atmosphere (too German, perhaps?), certainly not the liberal view of ideas. In 1943, Merle Curti, a social historian, turned his attention to American ideas. His *Growth of American Thought* was an instant classic, winning the Pulitzer Prize the next year. In the preface to the third edition, nearly forty years later, Curti explained his approach. "The original edition of *The Growth of American Thought* assumed that ideas could best be understood in terms of their social context and social utility.... It emphasized the role that the church, government, and business, the development of schools, publishing and libraries, the impact of wars and economic crises [have on ideas]." Curti admitted that he was well aware of the other tradition, linking ideas to one another according to their "philosophical foundations," and did not object to a fusion of his approach and the internalistic one. But the history of his times, of two world wars, a cold war, and totalitarianism with its manufacturing of ideas and compulsive adherence to certain doctrines, had convinced him that ideas cannot be seen apart from their contexts.[39]

Curti's was both a valuing of ideas in general and a proposal of how we should weigh particular ideas. But Curti was not particularly concerned about the truth of ideas. Unhindered by the long European tradition of internalist, philosophically defined intellectual history, and stimulated by the way that real life seemed to foster ideas in America, Curti democratized intellectual history. The substitution of thought, something everyone engaged in, for ideas, something for elite minds to conjure, was the tipoff. Curti brought everyone into the tent, not only by demystifying the study of ideas but also by crediting popular notions and ordinary thinking.

Curti's transformation of the notion of social ideas came just in time to save intellectual history in America. For part of the Red Scare of the period 1947–57 was an antipathy to "eggheads" and intellectuals. The actual connection between some literary, artistic, and scholarly figures in the 1930s with the American Communist Party became the hook on which "red-baiters" hung this anti-intellectual campaign. As Richard Hofstadter's *Anti-Intellectualism in America* explained, "[T]he intellectual, dismissed as an 'egghead,' and oddity . . . would be made the scapegoat for everything from the income tax to [the Japanese sneak attack at] Pearl Harbor." When not persecuted, the egghead was belittled and dismissed as ineffectual and effete. How better, then, to save American thought from the same fate than to associate it with robust national institutions like churches and schools?[40]

Fully reuniting history and philosophy is an uphill effort. As Ernst Breisach, a learned student of both history and philosophy, has reported, "Historians, for plausible reasons, have rarely responded with alacrity to opportunities to engage in theoretical debates." The divide had grown as academic training in the two disciplines diverged. D'Arcy:

> Most historians were not themselves philosophers and therefore they were not themselves aware of their own serious predicament; nor were they able to offer a well-considered and balanced defence of historical knowledge. They were not trained to meet those who challenged the historical method as inherently vicious and they had no philosophical knowledge to call upon when attacked by philosophers who trusted no other forms of knowledge save deduction and induction. This was indeed a situation which has continued even to this day.

To say that there is very little "interplay" between historians and philosophers of history today is something of an understatement, matched only by "historians are de-motivated regarding the study of philosophy of history."[41]

* * *

But history shares so many characteristics with philosophy that every historian should concede that the two disciplines are companions. For like philosophy, history is never quite done. Not only is there more to say, but each generation, each school, each student of the past refuses to accept any account or analysis as final or definitive—not for long, at least. So the historian endlessly revisits wars, movements, and individual lives in the same way in which philosophy revisits essential questions of human valuation. A truly philosophical history, then, is not one that deduces universal principles or unvarying values but one that celebrates the ongoing quest to know about the past, to know what is and what is not evidence, belief, and reality.[42]

[3]

History and the Social Sciences

The social sciences force themselves on each other, each trying
to capture society as a whole.

FERNAND BRAUDEL, *On History* (1969)

Religion and philosophy elevate history's humanistic qualities, the desire
and the ability to know more about ourselves, a collaboration whose
roots go back to written history's inception. But historical knowing has
a less yielding side as well, an inclination to scientific rigor. After all, to
say that history is a way of knowing this or that is to say that someone
is doing research into original or primary sources and finding evidence
to assemble into facts. Doing history is piecing together bits of evidence
to make facts and then selecting and arraying facts to make arguments
about what most likely happened. In the process, the historian makes
thousands of little mental leaps: Is this evidence reliable? Is it the best
evidence I can have for the story I want to tell? Have I rightly read the
evidence? Have I assembled the pieces of evidence in the right way? All of
these kinds of technical assessments precede larger conclusions about the
significance of events, the motives of people, the causes of movements,
and the meaning of the past. All of this resembles the scientific method.
One cannot put the past in a test tube or run laboratory measurements
on past events, but surely history's ability to understand the past should
be weighed alongside the other social sciences."[1]

Is History a Science?

The collaboration of history and the social sciences is a relatively modern one. The word "historian" became part of standard English only in the late Renaissance and at the time did not distinguish the student of history from the literary inventors of fabulous chronicle. At the outset of the seventeenth century, historians routinely invented speeches, freely incorporated rumor and gossip, included myths and legends, and did not check their sources as they do today. Indeed, the very notion of a historical fact, proven by the critical examination of evidence, was a product of later seventeenth- and early-eighteenth-century historical criticism. In its infancy, historical scholarship was no more scientific than any other contemporary intellectual endeavor when it came to judging the past. The producers and the consumers of historical tales were very much alike in the way they processed information.[2]

For this reason, the most learned man of his age in England had serious doubts about the scientific foundations of a subject like history. Francis Bacon was an Elizabethan and Jacobean English lawyer, judge, member of Parliament, scientist, philosopher, and essayist—in short, a true Renaissance intellectual. Though conventionally religious, he was highly secular in his outlook. Best known as the formulator of the "scientific method" and a practitioner of scientific experiments, he was as skeptical of the broadest claims of science as he was of those of law or religion. Never quite wealthy enough to pay for his expenses or powerful enough to satisfy his ambition, he nevertheless became solicitor general, attorney general, and finally Lord Chancellor under James I of England. He was impeached for corruption in 1621 and found guilty of taking gifts from litigants (a common practice) and other less common acts of immorality. He died in disgrace in 1626, all manner of rumor and accusation swirling about him.[3]

Bacon had an abiding interest in history and treated it as a subspecies of science—that is, he subjected written histories to the same sort of experimental categorization he imposed on natural or "mechanical" studies. He divided "civil history" into three types—uncompleted, finished, and defaced, likening them to portraits. The uncompleted memorial was a bare recitation of names, dates, and places much like the "CliffsNotes" used in high school classrooms years ago. They lacked analysis of causation and motive, surviving as mere antiquities, quixotic relics of the writers' own biases and interests. Ironically, much of what we know of Bacon's life came from *Brief Lives*, John Aubrey's late-seventeenth-century antiquary. Aubrey collected salacious gossip, spiced it with his own opinions, and served it in a broth of anecdotes. Bacon would not have liked the dish. Far more to his taste were true "histories," completed pictures of the "magnitude of actions, and the public faces and deportments" of important persons. But even these had "blanks and spaces" that authors felt free to fill with their own speculations. Of the decayed history, the false depiction—one thinks of the distance between Dorian Gray in person and his portrait—the less said the better.[4]

Historical writing at the time was prey to the "idols of the mind" Bacon warned against in his *Novum Organum* (1620). There were four. The idols of the tribe "have their foundation in human nature itself. . . . [T]he human understanding is like a false mirror, which, receiving rays irregularly, distorts and discolors the nature of things by mingling its own nature with it." The second, the idols of the cave, "are the idols of the individual man. For everyone (besides the errors common to human nature in general) has a cave or den of his own, which refracts and discolors the light of nature; owing either to his own proper and peculiar nature or to his education and conversation with others; or to the reading of books, and the authority of those whom he esteems and admires." The third, idols of the marketplace, arise from conversations among those who are not knowledgeable, "on account of the commerce and consort of men there. For it is by discourse that men associate; and words are imposed according to the apprehension of the vulgar." The last are the idols of the theater, "idols which have immigrated into men's minds from the various dogmas of philosophies, and also from wrong laws of demonstration . . . but so many stage-plays, representing worlds of their own creation after an unreal and scenic fashion. Nor is it only of the systems now in vogue."[5]

Elite and common consumers of history shared all of the idols of the mind. Popular culture and aristocratic culture were distinct only to the extent that the former was still largely oral while the latter was becoming increasingly written. As late as 1644 in England, for example, less than 20 percent of the total adult population could write, though many more could read. But literacy did not deter the educated few from indulging in the superstitions and enjoying the supernatural as much as the ordinary folk did.[6]

What would free the historical mind from these pitfalls, and elevate history above them? The answer seemed clear to later generations of scholars: associate history with science; or, go further—call history a science. The achievements of the scientific revolution in the period from 1600 to 1700 in western Europe wrought a gradual change in thinking about all phenomena. The experimental method the seventeenth century introduced in biology, chemistry, physics, and astronomy was a powerful challenge to intellectuals to rethink old theories of human nature. Perhaps more important, each new discovery in the various scientific disciplines spurred further discoveries. While science was still more demonstration than theory, the old distinction between theories of nature and practical or technological improvement was melting away. The same men who expanded the boundaries of theory, for example the English chemist Robert Boyle, also designed and built experimental models. The old brake on the publication of such findings, the power of the Church to censor books, was still there—witness the suppression of Galileo's astronomy—but in some locations, particularly England and the Low Countries, scientific publication was almost entirely uncensored. Experimental chemistry and biology were supplanting older notions of natural philosophy, a study of nature mixed with metaphysics, mysticism, and religious doctrine. The persuasive power of the new science, according to S. W. Serjeantson, was "greater than that of natural philosophy had ever been."[7]

The long shadow of the new way of knowing fell across the chronicler's page. Just as eighteenth-century Enlightenment science proposed that experimentation in chemistry and physics uncovered basic laws of nature, so eighteenth-century historians began to propose that politics and society obeyed their own natural laws. They were confident that

"Reason would rebuild the world of humanity, arming herself with the prestige of science, which we know from [Isaac] Newton cannot err." The parallel was not perfect. As the French student of government Montesquieu wrote in his *Spirit of the Laws* (1752), "The intelligent world is far from being as well governed as the physical world. For, though the intelligent world also has laws that are invariable by their nature, unlike the physical world, it does not follow its laws consistently." Nevertheless, the self-assigned task of the student of human history became to discover the laws of society and the state, and to explain any deviations from them in history. As the French sociologist Auguste Comte wrote in the middle of the nineteenth century, the study of the laws of society might still be in their infancy, but further research, observation, and compilation would surely raise the study of the past to a more reliable level.[8]

In the second half of the nineteenth century, when history was making its claim for a place in the new world of graduate schools, historians found the cachet of science almost irresistible. If history were a science, then its practitioners were not mere antiquaries and annalists. The French historian Fustel de Coulanges lectured his colleagues in 1862, "[H]istory is something more than a pastime . . . it is not pursued merely to entertain our curiosity or to fill the pigeonholes of our memory. History is and should be a science." J. B. Bury, a professor of history at Cambridge University, taught his students forty years later, "[I]t has not yet become superfluous to insist that history is a science, no less and no more." The library and the archive were laboratories, and historical evidence rigorously tested and objectively presented could be used to prove, or disprove, hypotheses about the past. In fact, for the first seminar room in the first graduate program in American history at the Johns Hopkins University in 1880, Herbert Baxter Adams adopted the science laboratory as his model.[9]

In 1927, the English historian and philosopher of history R. G. Collingwood formulated the most sophisticated version of the history-as-science view.

It thus appears that history is not doubtful at all. . . . [T]he question "what the evidence proves" [as opposed to what really happened] is not doubtful. . . . That question can be answered by a competent scholar, with no more doubt than what must attend any man's answer to any questions that can be asked in any department of knowledge. And in the certainty of that answer lies the formal dignity, the logical worth, the scientific value, in the highest sense of that word, of historical studies.[10]

The Rise of the Social Sciences

In tying history to science, the historian solicited the collaboration of the social scientists. In the nineteenth century the technological and mechanical application of the natural sciences transformed industry, commerce, and everyday life. The standard of living improved with advances in public health. Information moved faster following inventions in sound transmission. New kinds of scientists appeared in the academic world—social scientists—to explain how the world worked, and the social scientists' "new ways of understanding the historical world" claimed possession of a field that historians already cultivated.[11]

The first recorded use of the term "social science" linked it to its intellectual forebear, "moral philosophy." In 1824, William Thompson wrote that "Social science, the science of morals . . . requires not only of what is technically called morals, and political economy, but of the outlines of all that is known." Thompson cited Bacon's quest for universal knowledge as the goal of social science. For him and his fellow social scientists, knowledge of society could be illuminated "with scientific accuracy."[12]

The academics of the Gilded Age universities, a new phenomenon in themselves, welcomed the rise of "social science," and in their hands it probed the workings of politics, society, culture, and economics. Economists were the first to form a professional organization, in 1885, followed in 1902 by anthropology, 1903 by political science, and 1905 by sociology. Political scientists, sociologists, anthropologists, and economists trained in the new graduate departments of universities like Johns Hopkins,

Columbia, Wisconsin, and Chicago and published their findings in scholarly journals and the publications of university presses created for that purpose. Experts in these disciplines found jobs in government and colleges, and they tutored the next generation of social scientists. Although they had different subject matter, all of the social sciences focused on method and sought regularities and uniformities, much like the hard sciences of biology and chemistry, rather than the historians' focus on singular events and leading figures' actions. Social scientists moved away from religious explanations and moral judgments toward what they saw as more objective secular explanations of human behavior. The Social Science Research Council that these social scientists created in 1923 fostered and funded this approach to the study of human behavior and to the methods of science as well. At its core, "the devotion to science [was] . . . a high calling."[13]

By the middle of the twentieth century, the collaboration between social scientist and historical scholar proved to be a fruitful one in skilled hands. In two remarkable but now little-known and infrequently cited essays originally published in 1948 and 1956, respectively, Thomas Cochran, an economic historian, and Richard Hofstadter, an intellectual historian, made the connection between history and social science even more sophisticated. Cochran warned against too simple a narrative technique that mistook the surface account of events for their causes. A "lack of communication" had prevented historians from using social scientists' findings on deeper trends. The surfeit of documentary evidence might conceal as much as it revealed of these forces of change. Theories and hypotheses on groups, periods, and other general phenomena would integrate the individual story into more powerful explanatory statements of major shifts and events. Hofstadter added a more personal note about the importance of interdisciplinary studies. Social psychology in particular interested him, as it gave him another window in the minds and motives of American leaders. It afforded him "a fresh store of ideas" and that in turn permitted an "analytical" revision of conventional intellectual biography. Use of these did not transform the historian into a social scientist but made history richer and allowed the historian to better approximate the multiplicity of motives in real life.[14]

The ideal is a mutual respect—historians using social science theory to inform their research, social scientists relying on historians' findings to test and polish theory. But social scientists did not always follow the rules laid down by historians for using historical scholarship. Sometimes social scientists' dogged adherence to particular theories dictated results and proponents of the theory "mined" the sources to find evidence for their arguments. As Eric Wolf wrote in his *People Without History* (1982), "This severance of social relations from the economic, political and ideological contexts in which they are embedded" was coincident with the founding of the social sciences. Each of them "parcel out the subject [of human behavior] among themselves. Each then proceeds to set up a model" that supposedly explains objectively, but which is (we know from studying their history) "an ideologically loaded scheme." Wolf's warning is sound, but surely the remedy was more and better social science history. Insofar as they study human conduct in the past, social scientists must be guided by the historians' canon, but as the following accounts suggest, the social scientist is a very selective borrower from history.[15]

Geography

The most comfortable of all these partnerships, and the oldest, is that between history and geography. Geography is the science of the earth's surface, a subject of abiding interest to premodern mathematicians. The best known of these early geographers was Ptolemy, a second-century Roman who piled into his *Geographia* just about everything known in the early Roman Empire, to which he added his own ideas about the size and shape of the earth (he knew it was a sphere) and included his still-valuable instructions on how to draw maps. Ptolemy's contribution was equaled by that of the eleventh-century Persian Abu Rayhan Al-Biruni, who first calculated latitude and longitude. But the geography of Ptolemy and Al-Biruni was more than a calculating science. Ptolemy intended his work to guide travelers, and Al-Biruni put his ideas to work drawing maps of cities and regions. Their example reminds us that geography's great fascination for people is its practical utility. Thus it is wrong to regard geography as a pure science, and most universities locate their geography departments in the division of social sciences.

Historically speaking, even this placement is suspect, for the history of geography demonstrates how closely tied it was to history. The first works of history that survived, like Herodotus's, were also storehouses of geographical information. As the historians' knowledge of the world expanded, so did the information on geography they included in their works. This tradition, of embedding geographical facts in historical accounts, remains strong. One cannot write the history of Europe, for example, without taking into account the effects of human endeavor on the landscape and the reciprocal impact on human activity of climate, soil, topography, and other geographical features. "These physical conditions are of profound human importance. They influence every facet of life from styles of clothing and of architecture to the practice of agriculture."[16]

The partnership worked both ways. Contemporary maps and descriptions of geographical features are vital sources for historians. They exhibit the worldviews and information available to navigators and travelers. Cartographers catered to the expectations and needs of those who used or purchased the maps. For example, for maps of the sea lanes ship captains wanted accuracy, possible when latitude and compass readings could be added to drawings of coastlines. But maps of land masses often had a different purpose, claiming the land for a company or a sovereign, as well as showing distances, place landmarks, and survey boundaries. Chinese map makers of the premodern period were especially adept at this kind of map, introducing concepts of scale (with square grids) and direction and including topographical and economic detail. As Chinese trade and influence spread throughout Asia, the maps included more and more informative texts, themselves drawn from earlier archival materials. They "alerted the Chinese to external conditions that might affect the country's trade and security." This process of incorporation and transformation of information from outside China's borders continued well into the modern era.[17]

There are a number of geographical theories of history, theories in which geography determines who rules, how people think, and the utilization of natural resources. Sometimes called environmental determinism, the theories have something of the malodor of Eurocentrism. That is, they were designed to be or have been deployed as justifications for people from temperate zones (particularly northern Europe) to take control of and expropriate the natural resources and labor of people from subtropical or tropical geographic zones. Notable at the turn of the twentieth century were the ideas of Yale Professor Ellsworth Huntington that temperate climates promoted energy and higher levels of reasoning, while warmer, wetter climates induced torpor and servility and supported the racism of Latin American and African imperial ventures. Huntington had visited the Middle East and taught in Turkey before World War I and concluded, "The tropical climate of Africa and South America causes their living creatures to differ greatly from those of temperate regions." Characteristic of these regions, "The people, too, were found to have little in common with other races, and to be the most backward in the world." It would be best, then, according to Huntington, if "the more tropical portions" of these lands "would to-day be better governed, more prosperous and more peaceful than at present if they were held by an enlightened colonial power."[18]

The American historian Frederick Jackson Turner, a contemporary of Huntington's, was also an advocate of geographic theories of historical development. Turner was convinced that the vast expanse of relatively free land in North America during the early years of the new nation contributed to the individualistic and democratic character of its people. His so-called frontier theory of American history explicitly tied geography to political culture: "[T]he facts of geography were more compelling than arbitrary colonial boundaries." The land beckoned, and turning a wilderness into settlements stripped the European of his old cultural garments and clothed him in American homespun. As the frontier moved west, so did the democracy, creating new kinds of leaders and policies. "We have had to deal with the connections of geography, industrial growth, politics, and government. . . . American history is chiefly concerned with social forces, shaping and reshaping under the conditions of a nation changing as it adjusts to its environment. And this environment progressively reveals new aspects of itself, exerts new influences, and calls out new social organs and functions."[19]

But Turner, like Huntington, saw geography through the refracting prism of race. The true frontiersman was not Spanish-speaking, or dusky in color, or native to the land. He was an Anglo-Saxon, the highest form of northern European manhood. Turner effusively praised Theodore Roosevelt for his pro–Anglo-Saxon views in the latter's *Winning of the West* and himself shared these, publicly and privately. Roosevelt had prefaced his work with "We of this generation were but carrying to completion the work of our fathers and of our fathers' fathers. It is moreover a matter for just pride that while there was no falling off in the vigor and prowess shown by our fighting men, there was a marked change for the better in the spirit with which the deed was done." Turner saw himself and his America in the same light: The history of the west was the story of "Anglo-Saxon occupation." In his later years, Turner conceded that the melting pot of many peoples had its part in shaping American values, but he never disavowed his racialist bias.[20]

Theories like Huntington's and Turner's are still fashionable in some quarters, but historical geography has gone far beyond (and above) crude racism of this sort. The very best historical geographies are multi-perspective in nature, incorporating epidemiology (the study of epidemic diseases), linguistics, and the cultural history of cartography, as well as more conventional historical findings. Only "a wider lens and a shift in stance" allows the historical geographer the right perspective on the movement of peoples over the land. For example, Alfred Crosby's work on the Columbian Exchange (a term he introduced in 1972) is a superb antidote to Huntington's crude posturing. Crosby explained how the European portmanteau "biota"—the diseases, insects, animals, and pollens that Europeans brought with them to the Americas—were as important in the success of the imperial venture as armor and firearms. "These killers came to the New World with the explorers and the conquistadors." Native peoples who had no acquired immunities to pestilence that Europeans had lived with for millennia succumbed by the millions. European rats, cockroaches, weeds, pigs, and cattle despoiled native crops and paved the way for the colonization of the Americas.[21]

Political Science

The second-oldest of the social sciences, today called political science, goes all the way back to Thucydides of ancient Athens. His *History of the Peloponnesian War* was as much about the politics of the Greek city-states as about the diplomacy and campaigns of the war. It introduced a clear-eyed (no gods waging war on one another through human agents; no miraculous events) analysis of the causes and effects of the conflict. The path from Thucydides to the American Political Science Association, founded in 1903, is remarkably straight. Its aim was his: to foster the more precise study of the state in all its manifestations; as the first president of the APSA, Frank Goodnow, put it, "the practical and concrete" facts of state power.[22]

Historians like William Dunning, Woodrow Wilson, and Albert Bushnell Hart were early presidents of the APSA. Modern political scientists write history all the time, borrowing from historians' works for background and using primary sources of past events like legislative records, election returns, contemporary comment, diplomatic correspondence, interviews and oral history, and public speeches. Insofar as the political scientist uses the source material of history, the quality of the historical materials in his or her work depends upon the extent to which the political scientist accepts and employs the canons of historical scholarship.

Take, for example, the political scientist James MacGregor Burns's biographies of Franklin Delano Roosevelt, *The Lion and the Fox* (1956) and *Roosevelt the Soldier of Freedom* (1970). Both won major history prizes because Burns acted like a historian, seeking complexity and depth, weighing and balancing admiration and criticism, amassing factual material, and adding insights into personal and political motives, rather than just using episodes and words to make points about political systems. But at heart, Burns remained a political scientist in the old sense, a moral philosopher. As he wrote in his 2004 edition of *Transforming Leadership*, "I believe leadership is not only a descriptive term, but a prescriptive one, embracing a moral, even a passionate, dimension." One cannot speak of Gandhi or Roosevelt as leaders in the same way one would speak of Hitler as a leader. A leader is measured "by the supreme public values that themselves are the profoundest expressions of human wants: liberty and equality, justice and opportunity, the pursuit of happiness." Weighed in this scale, Hitler would not move the balance a fraction of an inch. While political scientists continue to make value judgments and look to the future (activities historians find unnerving), the two disciplines have a long and relatively comfortable relationship.[23]

Modern political science is no longer confined to the descriptive. Its quantitative face, for example, inspires historical studies of legislative and judicial behavior, electoral blocs, and public official behavior. Behavioral research itself has formulated models of great utility to historians. But the collaboration remained two-sided. Even when behavioral research is faulted in the political science academy for failing to reach deeply into the motives of public and private actors, political scientists have found historical records and analysis useful correlatives and correctives to empirical research methods. Typical is the "new institutionalism" school, revisiting the old political history with new insights into how governmental institutions gain lives of their own. Perhaps the best evidence of this continuing cross-fertilization, however, lies in the field of "state-building." Here historians like Brian Balogh and Williamjames Hoffer have built on the insights of political scientists like Stephen Skowronek to trace how the modern bureaucratic state evolved. It is hard to imagine a future for political science scholarship that does not continue its close ties with historical research and writing, and almost as hard to conceive of a political history that does not find use in political science findings.[24]

Cultural Anthropology

The origin of cultural anthropology lies in historical scholarship. David Hume, eighteenth-century Scottish philosopher, historian, and (though the term did not yet exist) social scientist, was the first cultural anthropologist. His "Of National Characters," part of his *Essays, Moral and Political* (1741), may seem antiquarian to modern eyes, but in it he attempted a science of cultural traits. It offers the same skeptical view of how culture works as his more famous philosophical tracts and the same common-sense observations as one finds in his histories. For example, consider his explanation of the origins of prejudice: "The vulgar are apt to carry all national characters to extremes, and, having once established it as a principle that any people are knavish, cowardly, or ignorant, they will admit of no exception, but comprehend every individual under the same censure. Men of sense condemn this undistinguishing judgment." Hume did not, however, revert to the older idea of the uniformity of human nature. Instead, he thought that political and social experience, added to natural circumstances, shaped "the peculiar set of manners" of peoples.[25]

The roots of cultural anthropology in the United States lie in the nineteenth-century study of Native American ethnic groups (called "ethnology"). North American Indians did not have a written culture, so students of their ways developed the technique of "upstreaming," learning about the Indian past by working with informants and focusing on oral culture. Modern cultural anthropology, the descendant of these first efforts, is still closely tied to history.[26]

Alas, there are some notable occasions when a preoccupation with a particular result caused a cultural anthropologist to misuse historical information. Nineteenth-century American cultural anthropologists found what they believed to be scientific evidence of the inferiority of African slaves and distorted the history of ancient peoples to try to prove the point. Mobile, Alabama, surgeon Josiah Nott found the racial theory of human descent compelling, and with the American Egyptologist George Giddon wrote the massive *Types of Mankind*

(1854) to prove the point. For both men, the history of ancient Egypt was crucial, but they ignored, denied, and fudged evidence that for at least part of that history, Africans ruled the Egyptian empire. They concluded instead that the "lower races of mankind" (the lowest of which were sub-Saharan Negroes) were inferior in intellect, moral perception, and emotional maturity, "all history, as well as anatomy and physiognomy prove this"—convenient findings for those who argued that slavery could only improve the condition of African Americans.[27]

The cultural anthropologist Ruth Benedict was well known and much respected among cultural anthropologists for her *Patterns of Culture* (1934), a sweeping synthetic comparison of the leading traits of a number of cultures. Influenced by her mentor Franz Boas, she did not look down upon Native Americans or African Americans as inherently inferior. But her analysis of Japanese society in *The Chrysanthemum and the Sword* (1946) misread Japanese history profoundly, out of a profound misunderstanding of how research in history worked. To be fair, she was working under the constraints of a war against a Japan that evinced Japanese indifference to the suffering of its own and other nations' civilian populations. But she was not a Japanese speaker or reader, nor did she delve into Japanese primary sources. To write "A Japanese who writes about Japan passes over really crucial things which are as familiar to him as the air he breathes" not only oversimplifies Japanese culture, it ignores the basic canons of historical research. Unable to read and understand spoken Japanese, unable to go to Japan in wartime, she relied upon Japanese who lived in the United States as informants. Just as the nonparticipant observer trying to understand a native society is dependent, so Benedict was confidently dependent on others, ignoring the ways in which contact with American culture, and the desire to please and influence her, would shape what her informants said. Again, Benedict's task was not an open-ended one. As part of the Office of War Information's effort to plan for the postwar period, she was to determine when a conquered and occupied Japan could become a trusted democratic ally. Predictably, she found that the Japanese, properly respected, would accommodate

American postwar needs. "When the Japanese believe themselves humiliated, revenge is a virtue. No matter how strongly Western ethics condemn such a tenet," the occupation forces must make every effort not to rub the defeat in the Japanese faces. For the Japanese were "a people of extreme situational ethics." After the catastrophic defeat planned for them, the Japanese would surely know their place in an American-supervised world order.[28]

At its best the discipline of cultural anthropology requires a kind of poetic imagination similar to idealistic history. The observer must be free to make leaps of empathy into the lives and beliefs of other people based on evidence not every historian would accept. Clifford Geertz, the foremost cultural anthropologist of the second half of the twentieth century, explained this poetic imagination thusly: using informants to tell stories about what happened in the past and then decoding the behaviors in the stories. Making actions and words into signs and then translating the signs as they fit into a pattern was what he called "thick description." The cultural anthropologist laid out "a multiplicity of complex, conceptual structures, many of them superimposed upon or knotted into one another, which are at once strange, irregular and inexplicit" and then "rendered" them intelligible to someone not from that time and place. But Geertz cautioned social scientists that cultural history, in their hands at least, was still "refractory" and "retarded." It was a challenge to do more with history and a recognition that history was vital to understanding cultures.[29]

Sociology

The other three social sciences most associated with history—sociology, economics, and psychology—are less inherently historical, but all three import historical evidence and write about historical subjects. Certain parts of sociology, the study of group behavior, roles, and relationships, may be entirely ahistorical, based on a series of cross-sectional observations or questionnaires. But even they have found a place in academic historical writing.

Indeed, the very founders of sociology as an academic field in the United States, in particular William Graham Sumner and Edward A. Ross, put history to use to defend their general theories of society. While it may be true that no historian or sociologist today would take Sumner as a model of method, he did introduce the first course in sociology, at Yale, and he continued to lecture on society and politics until his death in 1914. He introduced terms still in use like "ethnocentrism" and "the forgotten man." One must concede that he was one of the Gilded Age's foremost public intellectuals.[30]

Sumner's classic work *Folkways* argued that a people's customs evolved over the entire history of that people and could not easily be changed. At least, that is what history taught him. "The analysis and definition above given show that in the mores we must recognize a dominating force in history." In history, "folkways become coercive, all are forced to conform, and the folkways dominate the societal life. . . . Thence are produced faiths, ideas, doctrines, religions, and philosophies, according to the stage of civilization and the fashions of reflection and generalization." Profoundly conservative, believing that government could never change the nature of men and that laws could never improve a situation, no matter how dire, Sumner opposed progressive government, particularly attempts to relieve economic suffering. "The history of financial distress in this country" was full of such schemes for reform, and "no scheme ever devised" by reformers brought anything but "turmoil, risk, and ruin." At the same time, special interests, including those of capital, had proved equally corrupting to government and society.[31]

Ross, as influential in his day as Sumner, saw in the tie of sociology to history proof of the value and necessity of reform from above and below. In Ross's massive *Foundations of Society* (1905) that tie was central. For "social evolution" was in fact historical evolution, and history, instead of some vast eternal plan, was actually the accumulated acts that became "the sorted materials ready to the hand of the inductive sociologist." The sociologist's job, then, was to see in the myriad details the larger patterns of social relationships. "History is not, as many suppose, the quarry to which sociologists resort for their material. The records of the past . . . are common quarry for both historian and sociologist. The former explores them for events . . . the latter prizes most the humble facts of repetition . . . of domestic life, manners, industry, law, or religion." This was exactly what Sumner assayed, but Ross, tackling the same project, came up with very different results. Reform was as natural and as needed as the conservation of older mores. For example, the reform of divorce law "lay to the opening of doors to a feminine career and the relaxation of old beliefs which constrained woman to bear unmurmuring her yoke." Or the end of slavery, "the peace movement, the reform of punishment [for crimes against property], the rise of socialism," all of which were as natural as the ills they sought to alleviate.[32]

Ross shared a key concept with Sumner. They both believed in the dangers of race suicide, the degradation of the Anglo-Saxon peoples by infusions of inferior "blood." Ross was a founding member of the American Eugenics movement, an opponent of immigration from southern and eastern Europe, and an advocate of breeding of the "superior races." As he wrote to a fellow Eugenicist in 1927, "an interest in Eugenics is almost a perfect index of one's breadth of outlook and unselfish concern for the future of our race."[33]

Today, sociological concepts and terms like "role orientation" and "group orientation theory" are commonplace in historical analysis. In fact, a new kind of historical pedagogy based on roleplaying has become very popular. Using materials prepared for the classroom, history teachers ask students to take on the roles of important historical figures in a particular case, for example the trial of Anne Hutchinson for seditious libel. Using dialogue from actual historical records, the student players re-create the historical event. The re-creation is scripted in the sense that the students must act as though they actually are the historical personages. Although the purpose is to help students understand what the past was like, the exercise depends implicitly on the sociological concept that social structures limit and define the roles that people can play in any real-life situation.[34]

Economics

Economics, particularly modern theoretical economics, often pointedly ignores history. This tradition goes back to the Enlightenment agitation of Adam Smith in Scotland and the French physiocrats for an end to government impositions on free trade. For these theorists, economic study had a historical component, but the laws of economics, like the laws of physics, were supposed to be outside of time and place. The same faith in the iron laws of economics influenced the first American economic theorists. The most important of these in the first half of the nineteenth century, Francis Wayland, influenced politicians and jurists as well as other economic thinkers. He believed not only that *laissez-faire* was the best economic policy, but any interference with the operation of free markets was immoral. "The individual right to property and the profits earned from it are grounded in morality as much as economics."[35]

But there were academics who regarded history as more important to economics and derived from it a different lesson from Wayland's. Late-nineteenth-century economists like Richard T. Ely, a reformer like Ross, saw in the historical study of economics, particularly the relationship between labor and capital, a basis for reform. In Ely's *The Social Law of Service* (1906), history taught that economic ills like poverty were not the result of individual sin but of the failings of the economic system, and that the welfare of the people had always been the aim of all moral systems. "When the rich oppress the poor, and the strong make a prey of the feeble, then the nation is led away into captivity." The ill effects of unregulated capitalism had thrown its shadow over all the Western nations, but "the past generation has witnessed a marvelous growth of a feeling of brotherhood among the wage earners of modern industrial nations. Possibly when the history of the nineteenth century comes to be written . . . this will be regarded as the most marvelous feature of the second half of the century."[36]

Though Ely's prediction was wrong—the industrial unionization and welfare state policies promoted by reformers in the late nineteenth century did not bear fruit until the 1930s—his belief in the close ties between economic thinking and history was reasserted in the 1970s. In that decade, economic history practiced by economists blossomed. The result was a spate of books and articles using quantitative methods, like Robert Fogel and Stanley Engerman's much-read *Time on the Cross* (1974). The quality that makes any and all of these forays into social science good history and elevates their reading of the past is the way their authors adopted the historical method. As Fogel and Engerman opened their epic study of the economics of slavery, "what is not generally known is that the traditional interpretation view of slavery [that it was unprofitable and that slaves were more poorly housed, fed, and clothed than free workers] has been under intensive critical review for almost a decade and a half by historians and economists who are trained in the application of quantitative methods to historical problems." It was the collaboration of the historian and the economist that allowed masses of data to be organized for the first time, and for the data to be subjected to computer analysis.[37]

Fogel and Engerman's findings were the subject of a decade-long debate among economic historians and historians of slavery. The contestants met in panels and gave talks at professional meetings. Paul David, Peter Temin, Richard Sutch, and Herbert Gutman published a collection of essays, *Reckoning with Slavery*, to rebut every substantive claim, along with many of the statistical conclusions, that Fogel and Engerman reached. Gutman and Sutch concluded somewhat uncharitably that Fogel and Engerman's most important contribution was a proof of "the failure of quantitative methods to provide historical evidence when divorced from the qualitative methods of history." In the collection, and in a separate work, Gutman, a student of the slave family, raised both moral and psychological questions. For example, even if whipping was not so common, what was the impact on the slave of the master's untrammeled power to use corporal punishment? Whatever the shortcomings of their pioneering effort, Fogel and Engerman had forced the historians to look more closely at the aggregate data, to make comparisons between slave and wage labor, to model micro- and macroeconomies' dependence on slavery.[38]

Economic history, a cross-breed of the two disciplines, is taught in both history departments and business schools. It has its own journals, its own jargon, and its own following among scholars. The *Journal of Economic History*, for example, publishes articles on "money and banking, trade, manufacturing, technology, transportation, industrial organisation, labour, agriculture, servitude, demography, education, economic growth, and the role of government and regulation," and *Economic History Review* "aims at broad coverage of themes of economic and social change, including the intellectual, political and cultural implications of these changes." Ironically, a discipline that boasts of its breadth is divided between those who believe in free-market laws and those who believe in the struggle between labor and capital—a throwback to the nineteenth-century debates between *laissez-faire* advocates and Marxists. Some economic historians insist on inductive reasoning from case studies. Others believe that general laws of economic growth permit deductive reasoning. No social science is so riven by ideological quarrels as economic history, but the field itself flourishes.

Psychology

Formal psychological theory plays a small role in most historical studies. Psychology's first trained practitioners, called "alienists," were not major players in social science until the twentieth century. Still, pioneers of psychology like the psychoanalyst Sigmund Freud did not hesitate to plunge into historical studies, and one of his last students, Erik Erikson, contributed a classic if somewhat impressionistic account of Martin Luther to the historical corpus.[39]

Freud's *Moses and Monotheism* (1937) boldly explained the origins of ethics and religion in the psychoanalytic needs of the id, the ego, and the superego. For "Ethics . . . means restriction of instinctual gratification. The [Jewish] Prophets did not tire of maintaining that God demands nothing else from his people but a just and virtuous life—that is to say, abstention from the gratification of all impulses that, according to our present-day moral standards, are to be condemned as vicious." For Freud, the history of religion, at least that of monotheism, recapitulated the history of the maturing individual, as instinctual id drives for gratification bowed to the moral authority of the parent. "Here also it is the parents' authority—essentially that of the all-powerful father, who wields the power of punishment—that demands instinctual renunciation on the part of the child and determines what ... the child calls 'good' or 'naughty.'" The history of the race was the history of the developing ego of the child.[40]

Erikson's *Young Man Luther* is at once a psychoanalytic study of Luther's conversion experience and his later theological ideas and a tribute to Freud's earlier work. "When Luther challenged the rock bottom of his own prayer, he could not know that he would find the fundament for a new theology. Nor did Freud know that he would find the principles of a new psychology when he took radical chances with himself in a new kind of introspective analysis." For Erikson, student of Luther and Freud, "applied to Luther, the first Protestant at the end of the age of absolute faith, insights developed by Freud, the first psychoanalyst at the end of the era of absolute reason."[41]

Although some critics of a psychologically infused historical scholarship think psychoanalysis is the only kind of "psychohistory" and demean it as a latter-day version of "phrenology" (in which character is said to be deduced from cranial features), that criticism is certainly too broad. As Philip Greven has wisely written, "Historians can learn much from students of the human psyche, especially by becoming sensitive to the recurrent themes and patterns of feeling and thought that emerge from the discrete and confusing details of ordinary existence." Peter Gay, who has written both psychoanalytically inspired history and more conventional intellectual history, reminds us that psychoanalytic psychohistory is "an orientation rather than a specialty ... not a handbook of recipes but a style of seeing the past. ... Nor need it be reductionist. History is more than a monologue of the unconscious, more than a dance of symptoms."[42]

There are a great many more strands to psychology than psychoanalysis and thus a great many more possibilities for a fruitful union of history and psychology. There is, for example, cognitive psychology, with its emphasis on the way in which we process the report of our senses. Cognitive psychology teaches that we privilege the impressions that fit preexisting notions in our minds and dismiss or reformat perceptions that do not fit our preexisting notions. Our desire for cognitive fit has led us to misperceive the intentions and acts of our diplomatic partners and our foreign enemies. The study of personality and its companion, trait psychology, can also inform historical accounts. "This approach to the total study of the individual has come to develop a distinctive philosophy of human nature; that is, man's psychological attributes may be quantified." While such measurements usually take place in present time (protocols or inventories filled out by applicants for a job or volunteers in a study), analogous forms of measurement can be applied to individuals in the past.[43]

* * *

Social science asks the historian for rigorous empiricism. Historians cannot reproduce the past in a laboratory, but we can insist that any sound judgment be replicated by other scholars. Social science asks that conclusions be based on evidence. We can ask the same of historians—that they be well trained, do research in the appropriate fashion, and submit their methods, findings, and account to the scrutiny of other scholars in the same field. So a scientific frame of mind, setting out hypotheses without bias, is a quality that every student of the past needs in order to make judgments that deserve credence.

[4]

History and Literature

The domain of literature must be ever more widely extended
over the domains of history and science.

THEODORE ROOSEVELT, *History as Literature
and Other Essays* (1913)

At its best, historical scholarship respects religion, reconciles with philosophy, and embraces social science, permitting faith, reason, and science to join in historical judgment. But as Francis Bacon understood,
there are always blanks and spaces in the evidence that the historian's wit
and artistry must fill. Writing history is a literary act. Can and should
the canons of fine literature and literary criticism inform the historian's
powers of observation and reportage? Is history an art form? To be sure,
historians of art will remind us that different cultures and different time
periods had different definitions of a work of art. What seemed elegant
in one era may seem overly decorative or plain to a later observer. This is
called relativism, and a relativistic view of historical truth has plenty of
room for literary imagination. But whatever literary fashions might be at
any given time, history and literature cannot live apart from each other.

As John Clive, a historian of historians and an exquisite writer himself,
reminded his readers, "There is surely no need to stress the readability of
the great historians: all one has to do is to open their books." His point
was deceptively simple: We know artistry in history when we read it.
For example, follow Frederic William Maitland, a turn-of-the-twentieth-
century English legal historian, to the period before King Edward I and

the royal judge's yearbooks, as Maitland seeks evidence of the wholeness of English law:

> Beyond . . . there lie six other centuries that are but partially and fitfully lit, and in one of them a great catastrophe, the Norman Conquest, befell England and the law of England. However, we never quite lose the thread of the story. Along one path or another we can trace back the footprints, which have their starting-place in some settlement of wild Germans who are invading the soil of Roman provinces, and coming in contact with the civilization of the old world. Here the trail stops, the dim twilight becomes darkness; we pass from an age in which men seldom write their laws, to one in which they cannot write at all.

Or open *The Education of Henry Adams* and find the turn-of-the-twentieth-century American historian of medieval art just back from England, reveling in New York City's energy: "A traveler in the highways of history looked out of the club window on the turmoil of Fifth Avenue and felt himself in Rome, under Diocletian, witnessing the anarchy, conscious of the compulsion, eager for the solution, but unable to conceive whence the next impulse was to come, or how it was to act. The two thousand years failure of Christianity roared up from Broadway, and no Constantine the Great was in sight." I am tempted to reduce this chapter to a string of such quotes, conceding how inadequate my own prose is to convey this artistry. As the prize-winning historian James Goodman explained in his call for submissions to *Rethinking History: The Journal of Theory and Practice*, the best history was "history written by writers who, whether composing the most complex theory or the simplest narrative, are attentive to the ways that form and style shape substance, content, and meaning."[1]

Modern academic historical writing, striving for the plaudits of fellow academics, sometimes mistakes pedantic jargon for prose. For example, consider this apology for jargon written in jargon: "[A]s with other disciplines, art history has developed meta-languages, special ways of communicating with other people in the group. Within such meta-languages certain points cannot be made or can only be made in a roundabout or lengthy way. There are dangers that any specialized terminology may be inaccessible to a reader who has not learned it stage by stage." I lost my way trying to follow the dividing path of the points "that cannot be made or could be made." Which was it, I thought. Rest assured, the authors continued, "yesterday's academic obscurities are tomorrow's by-words." If only I knew what by-words to welcome into our already overstuffed vocabulary. Or this elegantly obscure approach to historical criticism through literary criticism: "[T]he heightened ambiguity of literary uses of language itself testifies to to the position of man in the world as a being who comprehends what he does not fully or conceptually know." How like the historian![2]

History as Literature

It is almost painful to compare the most egregious modern professional historians' jargon to the prose of the best-loved and -read of Victorian-era historians like Francis Parkman of Massachusetts and Thomas Babington Macaulay, a Briton. Parkman was Boston born and bred and Harvard educated and, though sickly much of his life, reveled in the strenuous pursuits of his New England forebears. He was very much a product of his place and time, believing in the superiority of New England Protestantism, Anglo-Saxon blood, and American patriotism.

For his multi-volume masterwork on the contest between the French and the English for control of North America, Parkman traveled the paths through the woods that his subjects traversed, trying to see the world as they saw it. In his later years, his eyes damaged from an injury he incurred at Harvard College, often confined to his Boston drawing room with the heavy draperies excluding the sunlight, Parkman hired a secretary to read to him the documents that his friends in Europe hand copied and sent him.[3]

The last of the seven tomes, published as two volumes in 1884, retold the final conflict. Parkman, by then all but blind, had not lost his ability to envision the meaning of the primary sources. Much of these came from the personal archives of the Marquis de Montcalm, France's premier commander in the French and Indian War. Of Montcalm's letters home, Parkman wrote, "No translation can give an idea of the rapid, abrupt, elliptical style of this familiar correspondence, where the meaning is sometimes suggested by a single word, unintelligible to any but those for whom it was written." Though this might seem the very definition of jargon, Parkman's description of Montcalm's prose was anything but jargon. And how typical this is of our letters to loved ones, for the code that bonds husband to wife and brother to brother, and father to child needs little elucidation and offers none to strangers. Note how Parkman captured the elusive style by matching it with his own, departing here from the ornate longwinded prose of most (including his own) Victorian histories. In a single passage, a work of art in itself, he captured the essential character of one of military history's most enigmatic figures.[4]

Where Parkman's sense of fairness failed, his pen did not. Consider his account of the Canadian Huron Indians.

He who entered [a Huron Indian longhouse] on a winter night beheld a strange spectacle. [The Hurons would not have found it strange at all—for them it was home, and a more sensitive historian would have realized this.] The bronzed groups . . . eating, gambling, or amusing themselves with badinage: shriveled squaws, hideous with threescore years of hardship; grisly old warriors, scarred with Iroquois war-clubs . . . damsels gay with ochre and wampum; restless children pellmell with restless dogs. Now a tongue of resinous flame painted each wild figure in vivid light; now the fitful gleam expired, and the group vanished from sight, as their nation has vanished from history.

He thought that the Hurons were superior to other Algonquians because of "the size . . . of their brains" (Parkman subscribed to the emerging pseudo-science of phrenology), but they were incapable of intellectual abstraction. Indian religion, for example, was "a chaos of degrading, ridiculous and incoherent superstitions." Finally, Indian character was morally deficient: "That well known self control, which, originating in a form of pride, covered the savage nature of the man with a veil, opaque, though thin. . . . Though vain, arrogant, boastful, and vindictive, the Indian bore abuse and sarcasm with an astonishing patience." No one who studies Native Americans today would subscribe to this racially bigoted assessment, but it is hard to deny the literary coup that Parkman achieved.[5]

Parkman carried on in the tradition created by the English Whig historian and politician Thomas Babington Macaulay. Macaulay was as public a figure as Parkman was private, helping to frame and pass the parliamentary Reform Act of 1832, lift the civil impediments against Jews, and serve in the House of Commons. In India, as a member of the British Supreme Council, he crafted a penal code that remains a part of India's laws. But the two men shared a love of words, the structure of their histories matching the subject matter. They would "embellish it with all the charms of the novel: lively narration, glowing description, that element of the dramatic—the sayings of the characters, and exposition . . . [proving that] the perfect historian should be an artist."[6]

Macaulay's great work, like Parkman's, was a multi-volume history of a critical period, England from the accession of James II in 1685 to the middle of the eighteenth century. At the center of the story was the Glorious Revolution of 1688–89. Then, Protestants and Catholics, parliamentary forces and King James II vied for the crown and the soul of England. King James knew that his Lords were plotting against him and came to believe that his only safety lay in the appointment of Catholic allies to key posts, particularly in Ireland. When members of his government protested his plans, "[t]he reply of James was dry and cold. He declared that he had no intention of depriving English colonists [in Ireland] of their land, but that as he regarded a large portion of them as his enemies, and that since he consented to leave so much property in the hands of his enemies, it was the more necessary that the civil and military administration should be in the hands of his friends." In a nutshell, Macaulay revealed the personality of a man given to passionate suspicions and strong-willed policies.[7]

Throughout his account of that critical episode, "Macaulay's habit of constructing his paragraphs by rounding off a tattoo of short, breathless sentences with a resounding period is more than . . . a trick of oratory, the surging and subsidence of thought in the orator's mind. Does not this stylistically reiterated sequence of tension and crisis leading to a climactic resolution reflect the critical and tense sequence of events" that Macaulay recounted? In fact, it did. "The relationship between style and content" elevated his work, as it did Parkman's, to the level of fine literature matching the novels of Charles Dickens, Thomas Hardy, and Anthony Trollope in England and Herman Melville, Nathaniel Hawthorne, and James Fenimore Cooper in America.[8]

Popular Historical Writing as Literature

The tradition of writing sweeping and elegant narrative prose for popular audiences is alive and well—alas, generally outside academe. One can find it on the history shelves at mass-market bookstores (while they survive) and on e-books. Popular history caters to popular interests. It tends to be upbeat—celebrating achievements, finding heroes, seeing in history the upward movement of civilization and the defeat of evil. Foremost among the profferers of this kind of history in the United States are Stephen Ambrose and David McCullough. Ambrose, a military historian and presidential biographer, and McCullough, best known for his biographies of John Adams and Harry Truman, are superb stylists. They tell stories about great events and great men. Their books sell in the millions of copies.

Ambrose was the most popular historian in America for much of the second half of the twentieth century. His biographies, adventure narratives, and World War II books are still staples in the bookstores. He told grand stories in vivid prose. Everyone was brave. For Meriwether Lewis, the expedition to the west with William Clark up the Missouri River, over the Great Divide, to the Pacific had revealed "a brave new world. And he had been the first. Everyone who has ever paddled a canoe on the Missouri or the Columbia, does so in the wake of the Lewis and Clark expedition . . . the journals of Lewis and Clark provided the introduction and serve as the model for all subsequent writing on the West." The same courage infused the citizen-soldiers of the D-Day American forces. Indeed, "this was distressingly close to the Duke of Wellington's sole requirement for his lieutenants, that they be brave." When it was revealed that much of Ambrose's work, from his Ph.D. dissertation to his final books, was riven with plagiarism, his public did not care, for Ambrose captured in prose the intense emotions of pride, courage, and idealism that the greatest of Americans shared.[9]

David McCullough was a writer and editor at *American Heritage*, a popular history magazine, when he began his career as a historian. He had no advanced degrees, no formal training, no pedigree in historical scholarship, but he proved that one could be a bestselling historian without any of those credentials. In 1968 his first book, *The Johnstown Flood*, appeared to rave reviews and excellent sales. He told the story of an arrogant elite building a dam for their hunting and fishing lodge and the terrible consequences that the bursting dam caused ordinary people downstream. McCullough had established a formula—the telling anecdote, the personalized vignette that fused good journalism and storytelling. His characters were a little larger than life and he plainly liked them. So did his readers. His subsequent volumes—*The Great Bridge*, on the building of the Brooklyn Bridge; *The Path between the Seas*, on the Panama Canal; *Mornings on Horseback*, a biography of Theodore Roosevelt; *Brave Companions*, a collection of seventeen biographical portraits; *Truman*; and *John Adams*, the last two of which earned him Pulitzer Prizes in biography, as well as National Book Awards—were all bestsellers. Typically, of John Adams McCullough wrote, "Dismounted, he stood five feet seven or eight inches tall, about middle size in that day, and though verging on portly he had a straight-up square-shouldered stance, and was, in fact, surprisingly fit and solid. His hands were the hands of a man accustomed to pruning his own trees, cutting his own hay, splitting his own firewood." How different from Parkman's Montcalm and Macaulay's

James II, but the method is the same: a few perfect brush-strokes and the inner character of a man becomes visible. McCullough is the voice of PBS's "American Experience" documentary series, and one could say that he was the voice of American history to viewers. (Though Civil War aficionados elect Shelby Foote's talking head on Ken Burns's "Civil War" documentary to this office.)[10]

The popular historians were popular in part because of their subject matter. They understood that the stories of great men and women, or the great deeds of ordinary men and women, were especially attractive to lay readers (about which more in the next chapter). But more important was their literary skill. They could make the past come alive. In this, they were joined by two academic historians whose works became popular though they were not originally intended for mass audiences. A public intellectual as well as a much-published scholar, Arthur M. Schlesinger Jr. hobnobbed with the great and famous, including a stint as the Kennedy administration's in-house historian. He won an unprecedented three Pulitzer Prizes, two for history and one for biography. His meticulous, balanced, and elegant biographies, political histories, and opinion pieces reflected a liberal worldview. Here he describes John F. Kennedy on the eve of his presidential run: "War had been a hardening experience. Politics hardened him more. Massachusetts Democrats did not exist as a party in the usual sense of the word. They formed rather a collection of rival tongs [Chinese gangs], controlled by local chieftains and presided over by an impotent state committee. Kennedy carved out his own domain and pursued his own goals. He showed himself determined, unrelenting and profane, able to beat the pols on their own ground and in their own language." There was no question where Schlesinger's sympathies or admiration lay in this paragraph (or in the rest of *A Thousand Days: John F. Kennedy in the White House*, for that matter), but re-read the passage and note the similarity to Macaulay: short sentences at the start, each sharp and to the point, followed by a closing sentence, a true resolving period—the whole paragraph capturing the energy of the moment, Kennedy's as well as Massachusetts' politics.[11]

When he died in 2007, the *Los Angeles Times* obituary reported that "Schlesinger in the first decade after World War II 'was . . . probably one of the two or three most influential historians of any sort' in the United States." Who can match Schlesinger's credentials: Harvard junior fellow in the days when "fair Harvard" shone above all other history programs; personal acquaintanceships with every major political figure of his day; and access to the media at all times? He was truly a successor to Macaulay.[12]

Schlesinger remained a liberal centrist in politics throughout his career. His great rival Daniel Boorstin moved from the far left to something in the middle of the right in American politics. Unlike Schlesinger, who welcomed the attention that celebrity brought, Boorstin was a private man, closer to Parkman in his inclinations. But Boorstin's intellectual appetite was enormous, his capacity to synthesize vast bodies of history unparalleled in historical writing. His books included a prize-winning trilogy on American history and wide-ranging surveys of European history, inventions, discoveries, and historical method itself. From his first book to his last, *The Seekers*, he had a gift for bringing history alive.

> Great seekers never become obsolete. Their answers may be displaced, but the questions they posed remain. We inherit and are enriched by their ways of asking. The Hebrew prophets and the ancient Greek philosophers remain alive to challenge us. Their voices resound across the millennia with a power far out of proportion to their brief lives or the small communities in which they lived. Christianity brought together their appeal to the God above and the reason within—into churches, monasteries, and universities that long survived their founders. These would guide, solace, and confine Seekers for the Western centuries.

The description could just as easily be applied to Boorstin himself. In the course of his long career, he won the Pulitzer, Bancroft, and Parkman prizes.[13]

Near the end of his teaching career, Boorstin was named Librarian of Congress, a position that, like the Archivist of the United States, carries great prestige. When Boorstin passed away in 2004, the *New York Times* accorded him a major obituary:

As the Librarian of Congress from 1975 to 1987, Dr. Boorstin literally brought drafts of fresh air into a stodgy, forbidding institution whose 550 miles of shelves and 19 reading rooms were all but terra incognita to the public and even to many scholars. He ordered the majestic bronze doors of the world's largest library kept open, installed picnic tables and benches out front, established a center to encourage reading and arranged midday concerts and multimedia events for all. Recalling his directive to keep the doors open, he remarked, "They said it would create a draft, and I replied, 'Great idea; that's just what we need.'" Dr. Boorstin, a man of prodigious energy who wrote almost every day, almost all the time, ran into a slight hitch at his Senate confirmation hearings. Several senators demanded that he not write while serving as the Congressional librarian. He refused to stop writing but promised to do it on his own time. And he did on weekends, in the evenings and on weekdays from 4 A.M. to 9 A.M. Witty, informal, a politically conservative thinker who favored bow ties and unconventional ideas, Dr. Boorstin provided America four decades ago with a glimpse of its reality-show and photo-op future, introducing the notion of the "pseudo-event" to describe occurrences, like news conferences and television debates, that are staged to get news coverage and shape public perceptions.[14]

Novelistic History

Popular history rivals historical fiction in sales and accolades, but of course history is not fiction. I am always taken aback when my students refer to works of history as "novels," not recognizing that the novel is a work of fiction. It all started with the novelist/historian Irving Stone.

About his smash hit historical novelization of the biography of Vincent Van Gogh, *Lust for Life*, Stone would write,

> The dialogue had to be imagined; there is an occasional stretch of pure fiction, such as the Maya scene, which the reader will have readily recognized; in one or two instances, I have portrayed a minor incident where I was convinced of its probability even though I could not document it, for example the brief meeting between Cézanne and Van Gogh in Paris; I have utilized a few devices for the sake of facility, such as the use of the franc as the unit of exchange . . . and I have omitted several unimportant fragments of the complete story. Aside from these technical liberties, the book is entirely true.

Aside from these liberties? If the historian has license to invent dialogue, embellish setting, and fabricate plot like the novelist, why should anyone trust the wisdom of historians? But surely does not the historian who has exhaustedly traveled all avenues of research have license to imagine what might have been in the blanks and spaces of the documentary record? I think so, if he or she clearly labels the filler.[15]

For some practitioners, the boundary between history and historical fiction is a semi-permeable membrane. As Eric Foner told the Key West Literary Seminar in 2009, "[T]he line between historical scholarship and historical fiction is not as hard and fast as we sometimes might think." Perhaps he had in mind John Demos's multiple-prize-winning book *The Unredeemed Captive* (1994). In it, Demos imaginatively recaptured conversations that must have taken place in some form or another but were not recorded. In the dramatic centerpiece of the book, a New England family is attempting to ransom a child back from the Indians who had captured her. In one passage, the girl's brother and she speak to each other through interpreters, she having forgotten her English, in a smoke-filled Canadian longhouse. "Perhaps it went something like this. . . . Smoke from the firepit stings their eyes. Voices float indistinctly toward them from the far walls. Human forms, a dozen or more, loom in the murk: squatting, lounging, bent to one or another little task. Slowly, one of the forms—no, two—move forward: a woman, slightly ahead, then a man. The woman draws very near, her eyes searching the three strange faces in front of her."[16]

We know from historical records that the meeting did take place, but its details are lost to us. Using the techniques of the novelist, Demos has filled in the empty spaces in the canvas. He admitted that he had taken liberties with the records, inventing dialogue for example, but argued that the historian, borrowing from the historical novelist, could fill in the missing evidence with educated guesses. From novels, as he reported in a 1998 essay for the *American Historical Review*, he learned the "strategies, the techniques, the 'moves'" to re-create a full-bodied past from fragments that survived. These enabled the historian to peer over if not cross the "boundary" between fact-based scholarship and fiction. The trick was to combine an almost excessive concern with those details that could be verified with a sense of the human condition—the ties that bound us to people in the past.[17]

Demos's attempt to use novelistic techniques to fill in gaps is useful when historians want to write about ordinary people. Most people do not leave much of a paper trail behind. In the past, when literacy was hardly universal and writing took time, effort, and the money to pay for paper, pen, and ink, ordinary people simply passed from view without a documented record of their lives other than birth, marriage, and death. But historians have found ways, artificial but effective, to bring these men and women back to life. Such pieces of exhaustively researched and engagingly written essays are called microhistories. The first of them was the Italian social historian Carlo Ginzburg's *The Cheese and the Worms* (1980). Part detective, part sympathetic narrator, Ginzburg recovered from legal records the story of Domenico Scandella, nicknamed Menocchio, a sixteenth-century Italian miller and local politician whose unorthodox views ended with his death at the stake. "He is always arguing with somebody about the faith just for the sake of arguing—even with the priest," one witness told the Inquisition. Another reported, "He will argue with anyone, and when he started to debate with me, I said to him, 'I am a shoemaker, and you are a miller, and you are not an educated man, so what's the sense of talking about it?'" Ginzburg allowed us to listen as Menocchio's neighbors describe him, just as if we were there, a literary alchemy turning the flat pages of the old documents into lively conversation.[18]

Novelistic history (to coin a term) not only has the pedigree of the nineteenth-century men of letters, but it is drawn from a tried and true novelistic technique. In *Tristram Shandy* Lawrence Sterne recounted the fictional life story of the title character, beginning with the events leading up to his conception. Periodically, he addressed the reader directly, commenting upon his own tale. Novelistic historians deploy the same literary device, pausing their histories to tell us how they were constructed. In his tale of the many histories of East Hampton, Long Island, Timothy Breen revealed, "I observe myself going about the business of interpreting the past out of a concern to let the reader know where I stand. . . . [H]istorians have a responsibility to converse openly with their readers." Breen was more than a chronicler in this story; he was a participant of sorts in the town's attempt to rediscover a lost past, but his reflections apply to all of us. In his remarkable survey of life among the woodlands Indians, *Facing East from Indian Country*, Daniel Richter did not cite Breen, but he assayed the same answer to history's impossibility. "So the chapters that follow are as much about *how* we might develop eastward-facing stories of the [Native American] past as about the stories themselves." He opened his book with three vignettes of encounters between Indians and European explorers, all from the now irretrievably lost Indian point of view. Hence, "these scenes are imagined." The more liberties the novelistic historian takes with the existing sources, the greater the need to "converse openly" with the reader.[19]

A final example of this literary method is somewhat awkwardly called "experimental history." All history is experimental in the sense that the historian cannot know her subject precisely; no history is experimental in the sense that a chemical laboratory procedure is experimental. No matter: To its exponents, experimental history "offered scholars new ways to develop argument and to convey complexity." It expanded the boundaries by empowering historians to tell a story from different perspectives at the same time, much as a novelist would. The attention to small details to make a scene come alive and engage the reader is not new, or even experimental, but the idea that history is a "conversation" that the historian and the reader overhear is also a borrowing from the novel. At the edge of experimental history lies the invented dialogue, based on what we do know and what we can surmise. We know that the dialogue took place, and we supply the words.[20]

History and Literary Criticism

In the turn to novelistic and experimental history, historians have sailed into turbulent waters. There lie the whirlpools and rocks of literary criticism. In the 1980s and 1990s, some intellectual historians took up the challenge of the so-called linguistic turn. They began to read and take seriously post–World War II "deconstructionist" and "postmodern" literary theories. The linguistic turn stressed the inherent complexity and uncertainty of texts, allowing readers to propose varying interpretations. (Perhaps inevitably given the academic origins of the linguistic turn, the adaptation of literary critics' ideas imposed another layer of jargon on historical writing rather than improve its clarity.) "Deconstruction" disconnected the historians' primary sources from their context and freed the language in the source from lockstep assignments of meaning. According to this linguistic theory, "All those old organizing frameworks that presupposed the privileging of various centers"—the "-centric" categories historians so love, like "Anglo-centric" and "ethno-centric"—were no longer representations of reality but useful (or harmful) "fictions" that historians manipulated. The intrinsic values or essences these centers supposedly represented (recall "philosophical history") were to have fallen, along with the certitudes they reinforced. No one belongs to a "ruling race," for example.[21]

While this critical program sounds ahistorical, in fact it spurred some historians to regard the words in their sources in a different light. "There is much to be learned from recent discussions of writing . . . concerning the productive quality of texts, their intertextual references and multiple meanings, their aporias, gaps and contradictions." Historical source criticism always asks if the source is reliable, biased, partial, or otherwise untrustworthy. Historians of literature, many of them professors of literature rather than historians, have always been especially concerned with structures of language. The postmodern historian joined the literary historian in looking at the internal relationships in the language of their sources, for many authors in the past were actually writing for one another, a kind of virtual conversation. "Conventional distinctions" between intellectual history and literary art were now all up for grabs, as historians asked whether the meaning of the terms in the documents they used had a one-to-one correspondence with some reality out there or were part of a self-contained system of signs whose meaning derived from use within the system. Predictably—after all, literary criticism cannot exist without literature—postmodern literary criticism provided more ammunition for those who claimed history as a branch of literature. This made the scientific quest for truth in history less likely and moved a literary kind of truth to the foreground.[22]

Despite, or perhaps because of, its close ties with literary theory, a too literal reading of the linguistic turn is highly suspect among professional historians. Joyce Appleby's admonition is gentle but telling: "After historians made that last turn marked 'linguistic,' they ran into same dangerous curves. Scholarly vehicles were totaled; avenues of inquiry left in disrepair. The timid got out their maps to look for alternative routes to the past; diehards demanded that the dividers be repainted." The irony of Appleby's caution was intentionally compounded when she chose an extended metaphor to follow the trail of the debate. But that was in 1989, and most historians have quietly moved beyond the extremes of postmodernism and the shrill debate over the linguistic turn, though the bashing of deconstruction and postmodernism in historical works continues.[23]

Although it may be true that "no one has ever provoked an objection by claiming history is a form of literature," for some students of the historical profession the attempt to liken history to literature is a form of desecration. That should not be so. Good writing is always in order. It does not free the scholar "to conceive of history as we will, and to adopt any perspective we please." Instead, it frees the scholar to reach more deeply into the very stuff that makes history a human artform.[24]

* * *

If history is a branch of literature and great historians merit our special attention, how does that reassure us about the historian's way of knowing? Great literature has the power to elevate our sympathies, enabling us to live lives not our own. It is cathartic, releasing our feelings in synchrony with the fates of the characters. It is a purging, cleansing, and ultimately purifying experience. Histories that bear the character of literature have the same cathartic power. When Montcalm faces his final battle on the Plains of Abraham, beneath the citadel of Quebec, we are there. In his tragic death defending French Canada we share an almost overwhelming sense of loss. When James II desperately plots to retain his throne, we watch in growing horror. Will he plunge his kingdom into civil war and ruin? When John F. Kennedy is struck by the assassin's fatal bullet, we cry out in anger and shame. Like Boorstin's seekers, we delight in the very act of human intellection.

History as literature lacks the compelling tone of religious, philosophical, and social science judgments. It does not tell us what or whom to believe or how to behave. Instead, it enables us to come into closer touch with those who have gone before us, to understand from within their virtues and vices. History as literature is a judgment in itself, a command to us to be a little more human. In this, it is the single most important way that the canons of fine writing inform and enliven the historian's task and make history more trustworthy.

[5]

History and Biography

There is properly no history, only biography.
RALPH WALDO EMERSON, *Essays:*
First Series (1841)

Biographers see themselves as a special breed of historians, concerned with how one person "lived, moved, spoke, and enjoyed a certain set of human attributes." Thus, of all the genres of history, biography is the closest to literature. This does not always bring the biographer a place in the front ranks of historians. "Consider how uneasily biography lies between historical writing and belles lettres." If, like the novelist, the biographer probes the hearts and minds of people in search of character and motive; if biography "humanizes the past," it also narrows that past to a single path. Biographers may explore the "inner life" of their subjects or emphasize the "public and social" world in which their subject traveled, but the subject remains a historical one. The synergy of biography and history is obvious.[1]

Everyone who ever lived has a biography. History is what happened to everyone, and everyone is part of history. The shop girl and the laundress, the dirt farmer and the truck driver are as much a part of history as the presidential candidate and the commanding general. Historians have developed social history, cultural history, the history of women, immigration history, urban history, labor history, historical demography, the history of the family, the history of childhood, and microhistory among other subjects of study to recover the lives of ordinary people. "We love to read the lives of the great, but what a broken history of mankind they give, unless supplemented by the lives of the humble. But while the great can speak for themselves, or by the tongues of their admirers, the humble are apt to live inarticular and die unheard."[2]

The "microhistory" is a popular modern form of biography that gives voice to the ordinary people. While the origin of these studies lies in Europe, European historians writing about European people and events on the margins of society (for example, Menocchio), the term has gained a somewhat different connotation among American historians. It has become synonymous with the biography of ordinary men and women. The best known of these, and the model for the genre, is Laurel Thatcher Ulrich's *The Midwife's Tale*, a brilliant and moving depiction of the life of a rural Maine midwife. Ulrich's literary skill transformed a slender and terse diary of midwife, mother, and businesswoman Martha Ballard of Hallowell, Maine, into a source that enables us to imagine the entire range of women's activities in early modern New England. We feel the cold of the winters' nights and the rough textures of homespun. What had been overlooked by historians for its terseness, Ulrich turned into a marvelous source, though, "One might wish for more detail, for more open expressions of opinion, fuller accounts of medical remedies or obstetrical complications, more candor in describing physicians or judges, and less circumspection in recording scandal, yet for all its reticence, Martha's diary is an unparalleled document in early American history. It is powerful in part because it is so difficult to use, so unyielding in its dailiness."[3]

Greatness in Biography

Ballard was a remarkable women in her time and Ulrich's account is a remarkable achievement, but what attracts most readers to biography (unlike what attracts many modern historians to microhistories of ordinary people) is what elevates human action above the ordinary. Greatness is not quite the same as common fame (and infamy). Greatness inspires us. Infamy disgusts us. But such distinctions are not as important to the connection between history and biography as those between the great and the common. For even before historians commenced their democratic voyage of discovery into the lives of the not-so-rich and not-so-famous, chroniclers' stock and trade was retelling the deeds of the great and the would-be great: stories of saints, kings, battles, and empires. In the nineteenth century, this notion was encapsulated in the "great man theory of history." Great men made history, and their example was the proper object of historical study. As Ralph Waldo Emerson wrote in "The Uses of Great Men," "Nature seems to exist for the excellent. The world is upheld by the veracity of good men: they make the earth wholesome. . . . We call our children and our lands by their names." The most popular biographer of that period, Thomas Carlyle, argued in his *Heroes and Hero Worship* (1869) that heroic deeds would live on in history forever. At the core of these narratives was the notion that there was a certain ineffable quality in people that historians and their readers could judge, a quality of greatness.[4]

The great man or representative man theory of history was the original foundation for biography and remains so. As the biographer John Morton Cooper Jr. explained his own choice of subjects, Theodore Roosevelt and Woodrow Wilson, "there is always the requirement that our subjects have historical significance and that they illuminate important things about the times in which they lived and the events in which they participated." In other words, the proper subjects of biography for most readers are those individuals in whom there is the quality of greatness.[5]

Biographers have sought this elusive quarry from the beginning of the genre. The first and foremost biographer of the ancient world, the Greek Plutarch was consumed with curiosity about greatness. Plutarch lived most of his life in Greece, though he traveled as an ambassador throughout the Mediterranean and attained Roman citizenship during one of his two stays in the imperial capital. In his native land, he held priestly and civil offices and had access to archives there and in Rome. As well, he was welcomed into leading families' homes. One might say that he was as much a historian for his age as Arthur Schlesinger Jr. was for ours, a celebrity author, raconteur, and pundit. "The charm of his style and the breadth of his vision of a past which had already become classical in his own day . . . won him admiring readers from his contemporaries to the present."[6]

Plutarch's judgments were often severe. As he wrote of Julius Caesar, the greatest figure in the Roman Republic after he had driven his rivals from Rome and amassed almost all power in his own hands:

> Caesar was born to do great things, and had a passion after honor, and the many noble exploits he had done did not now serve as an inducement to him to sit still and reap the fruit of his past labours, but were incentives and encouragements to go on, and raised in him ideas of still greater actions, and a desire of new glory, as if the present were all spent. It was in fact a sort of emulous struggle with himself, as it had been with another, how he might outdo his past actions by his future.

Not content with conquest of Gaul and Egypt, he eyed Germany and Thrace, and beyond. There was no limit to his desire for conquest and fame.[7]

Plutarch's *Parallel Lives* of famous ancient Greeks and Romans was an exploration of the quality of greatness. By comparing lives, he sought to isolate the trait. Caesar was great, but corrupt and venal. Merely possessing power did not ensure true greatness, a quality that eluded Caesar in Plutarch's judgment. Instead, true greatness was elevation of spirit, as Plutarch implied when he compared the modest but intensely serious Athenian orator Demosthenes with the boastful and jokingly eloquent Cicero of Rome. Both men opposed tyrants, Demosthenes denouncing Philip of Macedon and Cicero attacking Mark Anthony. Both men were banished and ultimately paid for their courage with their lives. For Plutarch, Demosthenes was the greater man because of his "gravity and magnificence of mind," compared with Cicero's tendency to "admire and relish" his own abilities. To Plutarch, true greatness required nobility of spirit.[8]

Like Plutarch, scholars and readers both want to know how to judge greatness, to know, in effect, who should be adjudged great. Nobility of the sort that Plutarch described is not the same as fame. One can be famous, for example Elvis Presley, without being great in spirit or grace. The ill fame of tyrants, for example Adolf Hitler and Josef Stalin, would surely elevate them as major figures in history, but to call them great men would be to stretch the definition of nobility past all imagination. We admire the great because we see something in them that we would like to see in ourselves. Today only the homicidal or the insane would see in monsters like Hitler and Stalin something of themselves.

The question then is not the definition of greatness but whether the definition is objective or subjective. For a great many Germans in Nazi Germany and others who watched the rise of Hitler with admiration, the man was the very epitome of greatness. He often spoke and wrote of it, and saw himself as the very personification of the greatness of the German-speaking peoples. With this in mind, one can ask if the definition of greatness is so elastic, so dependent on time, place, and the situation of the speaker, that one observer's great person can be another avatar of evil. In other words, is greatness subjective?[9]

The Subjectivity of Greatness

A series of case histories will help to answer the question of how to determine greatness. Take the membership application of one Christopher Columbus. Does he belong among the greats? Samuel Eliot Morison certainly thought so, and Morison was a giant among historians in the first half of the twentieth century. Boston and Harvard prepared him for the life of a scholar, and a stint as the historian of the U.S. Navy in World War II turned his attention to Columbus. Morison's *Admiral of the Ocean Sea: A Life of Christopher Columbus* won the Pulitzer Prize in biography for 1943. His Columbus, fittingly, "would be the humble yet proud instrument of Europe's regeneration . . . [W]ith a maximum of faith and a minimum of technique, a bare sufficiency of equipment and a superabundance of stout-heartedness, [he] gave Europe new confidence in herself, more than doubled the area of Christianity, enlarged indefinitely the scope for human thought and speculation, and led the way to those fields of freedom which, planted with great seed, have now sprung up to the fructification of the world." Case closed?[10]

When I was a pupil at P.S. 188 in Queens, many years ago, we celebrated Columbus Day, October 12, the day he and his crew arrived in the Bahamas. The celebration closed the schools, and there was a parade down Fifth Avenue in Manhattan. No one doubted for a second the greatness of Columbus. No one thought that his greatness was a subjective judgment. As the five-hundred-year anniversary of Columbus's first voyage approached, President George H.W. Bush prepared the way for a national festival commemorating Columbus's arrival in New World waters. "On Columbus Day, we pause as a nation to honor the skilled and courageous navigator who discovered the Americas and in so doing, brought to our ancestors the promise of the New World."[11]

Little did the president anticipate that the quincentenary celebration in 1992 would cast Columbus and his fellow European explorers in a wholly new and not very flattering light. For every parade that year, there was a protest. Native American groups called the coming of Columbus the beginning of centuries of genocide. The American Library Association resolved: "[W]hereas Columbus's voyage to America began a legacy of European piracy, brutality, slave trading, murder, disease, conquest, and genocide"—a very different tack from the president's proclamation. The U.S. Congress's Columbus Quincentenary Jubilee Commission tried to quiet the dispute by changing the "celebration" to a "commemoration," but the shift in language mollified few of Columbus's critics or defenders.[12]

Did not Columbus deserve a better fate? Did he not prove the world was a sphere, and that sailing to the west would bring him to the Western Hemisphere? Had he not discovered America and brought with him civilization and prosperity to benighted and primitive native peoples? Actually, nothing in these statements is quite true. He was not the first to see the earth as a sphere. Ptolemy, the Greek geographer, did that during the early Roman Empire. Renaissance scholars had rediscovered his work, kept alive in Arab libraries, and republished his maps in 1477. Columbus, trained as a ship's navigator in Portugal, knew all about these maps, though he (like Ptolemy) misjudged the size of the earth by a third.[13]

The name America came from one of Columbus's rivals, Amerigo Vespucci, something of a scalawag. Vespucci, an Italian map maker and explorer, visited the coast of South America in 1502 and 1504, but his original accounts are lost, and what was published under his name is probably fabulous. He scooped Columbus by accident, only because a German map maker and printer named Martin Waldseemueller needed a name for the places that Vespucci said he visited. The Americas became continents on the map of the globe Waldseemueller was preparing.[14]

Nor did Columbus think he had discovered the Americas. He believed to his dying day that he had come to the edge of Asia, where the East Indies and their wonderful spices were to be had, and for this reason he called the natives he encountered Indios. In fact, he was not the first person to arrive in America. Archeological evidence puts the first Americans on the continent more than 15,000 years ago. In fact, in the Indies Columbus met relative newcomers to the Bahamas. The Taíno peoples had arrived only a few hundred years previously. As Samuel Eliot Morison's Pulitzer Prize–winning biography concluded, "except for a few prophetic moments, it was Columbus's misfortune to ignore the significance of his discoveries that have given him immortal fame, and to advance geographical hypotheses that made him a laughingstock for fools."[15]

As for civilized gifts from Europe, when Columbus came to the Americas he brought with him cockroaches, rats, smallpox, chickenpox, measles, and weed pollen. His livestock, notably the pigs, destroyed Indian crops. In their search for gold, his men despoiled Indian villages and took Indian lives. Islands in the West Indies whose populations before Columbus approached one million were reduced to the thousands by 1520. Columbus was no godsend to the Indians.[16]

But perhaps Columbus is still rightly judged a great man by Plutarch's old standard. Though not an aristocrat, he had a certain nobility of spirit, the gumption and the ability to convince a foreign potentate (the queen of Spain) to finance a three-ship voyage. He kept a near-mutinous crew in check during that voyage. He was a fine blue water sailor and an even better navigator of treacherous coastal shoals. Dubbed by Queen Isabel the "Admiral of the Ocean Sea" after he returned from his first voyage, Columbus led three more fleets on voyages to the Bahamas, the Caribbean, and the coasts of South America and the Gulf of Mexico. To the court of Spain, and from thence all over educated Europe, Columbus brought evidence of strange and wonderful people, plants, and animals never seen in the Old World. With these came the promise of great riches. Spain, and later its European rivals France, England, Portugal, and the Netherlands, would exploit those riches, leading Europe on the path to imperial power and wealth. For Europe in the Americas, it all started with Columbus. "The true importance of his discovery became clearer with every passing decade as the New World yielded up its considerable treasure to the Old, and as the historical significance became appreciated in scholarly, and then popular, opinion."[17]

If greatness in history is a matter of influence, then the elusive quality of nobility need not be sought. One could propose an objective definition. At its most basic, the formula for greatness would be: Whoever changes the course of history the most is the greatest figure in history. Indeed, under this definition more often than not it is the bad man who is great, for ambition, greed, and hunger for power sometimes prove far more potent motivations than loving kindness and serenity. Thus would a paradox lie at the center of biography—history may attach objectively greatness to those we most abhor.

One cannot accept the simple idea of greatness equaling influence, however, because no one can change history unless the times are ripe for change and that person's abilities fit the time and place—a sort of Darwinian definition of greatness. But as in Darwinian evolution, fitness is a matter of fit. The times must be right for the individual's own gifts and vision to make an impression on those times.

Consider then the American schoolmaster James Johonnot's *The Ten Great Events in History* (1887). Chapter 5 introduced Columbus.

Columbus lived in a stirring age. Everywhere light was breaking in after centuries of darkness, and all Europe was restless with suggestions and beginnings of new life. Great men were plenty; rulers, like the Medici of Florence . . . reformers, chief among them Luther, just beginning to think the thoughts that later set the world agog. Great inventions were spreading . . . suddenly opening knowledge to every class; the little compass, with which mariners were just beginning to trust themselves boldly on the seas, in spite of the popular impression that it was a sort of infernal machine presided over by the devil himself.

A rising tide of greatness lifted all boats, Columbus's boats, and America's, for it was to America that Columbus carried the genius of his age, the Age of Discovery. Columbus brought the energy, intelligence, and will of Europe to America. In the heady days after the celebration of all things American after the triumph of the Centennial International Exposition of 1876 in Philadelphia, it was comforting for Americans to know that the origins of their nation went as far back as Columbus's heroic deed.[18]

Columbus was great not only because he was a heroic figure. He was also a representative figure to turn-of-the-twentieth-century biographers. He joined a list of eminent men in Rossiter Johnson's twenty-volume set of *Great Events by Eminent Historians* because what he appeared to represent was important to biographers then. It was an age in the West that celebrated invention, exploration, and Western ideas. Some of these may seem above reproach today—material improvement, progress, and science. Other notions the biographers lauded may seem repellent—racism and imperialism, for example. Johnson linked the two sets of concepts. "As the surveyors of a great country take their observations from hilltop to hilltop, and thence make the triangulations that reveal the extent and character of the lower ground, so may one read history to the best advantage—first from the altitude of great and significant events, such as turn the course of empire or hasten the march of civilization." For only through the celebration of true greatness would Americans see that they were the true inheritors of the ruling races. From the work of "a carefully elaborated list of authorities throughout America and Europe" Johnson derived "the following practical, and it would seem incontrovertible, series of plain facts," the triumph of the Western European man over lesser peoples and more primitive cultures.[19]

Biography would prove what history surmised: "When our human-kind first become clearly visible they are already divided into races, which for convenience we speak of as white, yellow, and black. Of these the whites had apparently advanced farthest on the road to civilization." Each race had its place, its characteristics, and its contributions, and according to the contributors to Johnson's anthonlogy these contributions were not equal. "Let us look at the other, darker races, seen vaguely as they come in contact with the whites. The negroes, set sharply by themselves in Africa, never seem to have created any progressive civilization of their own, never seem to have advanced further than we find the wild tribes in the interior of the country to-day." The prosopography of *Great Events* was rooted in racism. It was to the Aryan race that Europe owed its eventual world dominion. Great events, it would seem, were the doing of great men, and greatness in men was determined by bloodlines, at the top of which was "our own progressive Aryan race."[20]

Johnson was an amateur biographer, but graduate school training and academic stature did not make a difference in the subjectivity of Victorian biographers' view of greatness. In 1890, John Jay, president of the American Historical Association, told its members that the nation owed its greatness to "the stronger races." After all, "the army of Washington were representatives of races which had been the most distinguished in the battle-fields of Europe . . . of the Englishmen who had battled at Naseby and brought the king to the block at Whitehall; of those who stood with William of Orange or with the partisans of James at the battle of the Boyne." It could not have escaped his audience that all of these heroes were Protestant, white, and from northern Europe—the same heroes who fought alongside George Washington during the war for independence (ignoring the French Catholics, the free African Americans, and the Indians).[21]

When time and place allowed, biographers could and did judge the connection between greatness and race differently. By the second decade of the twentieth century, the Indian wars were over. Sitting Bull, once a feared adversary, toured with Buffalo Bill Cody's Wild West show. Geronimo had spent his last days in exile in Florida, more than 2,000 miles away from his native Arizona. No longer a threat to the westward movement of the ruling races, Indians' nobility could be attributed to racial characteristics in the same way that Indians' ferocity was once attributed to immutable racial character. For example, Ely S. Parker, a Seneca Indian leader, after training as an engineer was taken on to U. S. Grant's staff (despite the general ban on Indians in the Union Army). Parker went on to distinguish himself during the Civil War (he was the draftsman of Lee's surrender terms at Appomattox) and as Superintendent of Indian Affairs during Grant's first administration as president. In 1919, the Buffalo, New York, historical society devoted an entire issue of its collections to a biography of Parker by his great-grandnephew, Arthur C. Parker. The preface to the volume, by Frank H. Severance, a trustee of the historical society, reminded readers "but the notability of Ely S. Parker, was and is unique, for he embodied in his life and his career the best traits of a race, always imperfectly understood and usually unfairly judged by their white neighbors. He was a high type of the Iroquois." Severance's was a kinder, gentler racism than Jay's.[22]

Such judgments are more than suspect. Because they are self-serving—Jay was a member of the stronger race, the master race, the ruling race—his views cannot be accepted without question. Severance could celebrate the nobility of the Seneca hero, for Parker was part white, from "clean honest stock," and that, added to the natural nobility of the warrior race (now safely confined on a reservation), made Parker a tribute to his people. Of course, in 1890 or 1905 or 1919 the science of genetics was in its infancy. Scientists recognized evolution but did not know how traits were passed. Thus skin color and hair type looked much more important then. Now science knows that the human genome is complex and that skin and hair types are not what make us human, much less what determine the course of history.

One lesson of the posthumously discovered greatness of an Ely S. Parker is that biographers' weighing of greatness is bound up in their judgment of everything else. In other words, they see the past through the eyes of their present. How could they pronounce so confidently about a ruling race in 1900, and then just as confidently pronounce today about the irrelevance of race? After all, Parker was forgotten when he died, in 1893.

Objective Greatness?

What if one were to begin the inquiry into the nature of greatness by selecting a consensus figure, someone whose nobility of spirit and whose influence on the course of history were not in question, and then asked how that reputation rose above the whim of biographers or the time and place of the biography? First, one would have to look for such a person outside the realm of biography. Otherwise the inquiry would be circular. The most obvious and the most simplistic of biographical judgments of greatness is public opinion. For little more than ease of presentation, we may consider polls ranking American presidents as an example of public opinion that can be tracked over time. By looking at the rankings at different points in time, one might discover an individual who different generations of American historians agree is great. That is just what happens. The first of these polls was organized by the Harvard historian Arthur M. Schlesinger Sr. in 1948. He asked historians whom they ranked at the top, and Abraham Lincoln was the consensus. In 1962, Schlesinger's son conducted another poll of historians. Again, they selected Lincoln. More recent polls of a broader spectrum of respondents (after all, how representative are academic historians?) show Lincoln's remarkable persistence at the top of the lists. His staying power through more than sixty years of polls suggests that there may be a consensus (if not an objective) measure of greatness after all.[23]

A closer look at biographies of Lincoln will show how an objective measure of greatness can shine through the haze of subjective viewpoints. When the nation was celebrating the bicentennial of Abraham Lincoln's birth, the hoopla was accompanied by several new books on the character, the politics, and the wisdom of Lincoln. Some commentators compared newly elected President Barack Obama to Lincoln, a connection made possible by Lincoln's wartime emancipation of slaves in rebel territory. How different this was from 1860, when Lincoln won the highest office in the land. Then, Americans had no difficulty deciding who belonged in the temple of greatness, and Lincoln appeared to have no chance to enter. Reviled by Democrats, sneered at by southerners, and dismissed by editors, politicians, and lay people in his own Republican Party, Lincoln seemed the wrong man for the momentous job ahead. To his great rival, Democratic presidential hopeful Stephen A. Douglas, Lincoln was small-minded, happy to incite "a war of sections," and a Negro-lover. To Mississippi's Jefferson Davis, Lincoln was a man who could not be trusted to obey the Constitution. He had no honor and was ruled by expediency. Davis's animadversions were mild by contrast with other southern fire-eaters. Yet all of the bicentennial celebrants, scholars included, had no doubt that Lincoln was great, a man whose resolve and genius led a nation in its darkest time. "Lincoln is revered as our greatest president, but he is certainly more than that. He is an unparalleled national treasure, a legend that best represents the democratic ideal. Every generation looks to Lincoln for strength, inspiration and wisdom." One of America's most beloved poets, Carl Sandburg, wrote a six-volume elegy on Lincoln. It ended with his death, as "To the four corners of the earth began the spread of Lincoln story and legend . . . mystic shadows and a bright aura gathered around Lincoln." The present count of Lincoln books is 775 titles, a surfeit added by the end of Lincoln's bicentennial.[24]

Perhaps our quest for objective judgment is too quixotic. We can, however, move past the differences of opinion listed above by recalling that any measure of greatness must involve both the individual and the times. Revisit those times. Lincoln served as president during the most horrific and perilous of all American wars. His life, until the Civil War erupted, did not seem to prepare him for greatness. But it did prepare him for suffering. Often lonely, beset by images of his dying mother, melancholy and depressed, he identified with others' suffering. Suffering taught Lincoln to hide a portion of his thoughts and feelings, and the empathetic suffering he exhibited during the war. The poet W. H. Auden wrote, "Let us honour if we can; The vertical man; Though we value none; But the horizontal one." Is Lincoln great because he is gone? Did martyrdom bring him glory? Is his mystical legend, as Sandburg termed it, more important than his actual life? Did death turn a skilled politician into a statesman? Elevate a meddling commander-in-chief into a master strategist? Transform a racist into an avatar of racial justice?

More questions, no answers. In order to understand the puzzle that Lincoln's greatness presupposes, one must once again ask how history determines greatness. One finds that in life Lincoln's reputation was not what it became after his death. True, a half-century after Lincoln went to his grave, he had become "the icon of American democracy." When going to the movies became the country's most popular pastime, Lincoln appeared on the silver screen as a young hero (*Young Mr. Lincoln*) and as an avatar of freedom (*Abe Lincoln in Illinois*) and the moving force behind the Thirteenth Amendment (*Lincoln*). But Lincoln's reputation in the scholarly world had as many ups and downs as Lincoln's own life. Reviled by some historians as the most egregious example of a "blundering generation" of self-interested and short-sighted politicians by some, defended as wise and practical by others, Lincoln remains something of an enigma.[25]

A final effort to judge greatness will rest on our own measure of the man. Who was Lincoln that we should be mindful of him? Born into a farming family, losing loved siblings and mother early, working his way up from farm hand to store owner to lawyer (and a very successful one at that); moving from place to place (the great passion of many in his day) to better himself; grasping at book learning with a kind of avidity that only his love of politics rivaled; settling into a tumultuous marriage that nevertheless worked for both him and Mary Todd; finding that politicking came easy but staking out an anti-slavery position early that barred his way to the leadership of his first party affiliation; stricken with bouts of depression and self-doubt but facing the world with geniality, modesty, and self-deprecating humor, Lincoln represented the antebellum white male. In him resonated all of the dreams, dashed and realized, of his generation. Though he decided to take a leading role in the quarrel that divided that generation, his role was scripted by the values of his fellow Americans. Their expansive ambition was his own. Their ambiguous moralism was his own. His part in the new Republican Party, his election to the highest office, his choice of cabinet, and his management of the war made him the most important man in America because he was everyman, and yet he controlled the lives of millions of men in uniform, a budget of billions (in today's dollars in the trillions), and a burgeoning federal bureaucracy. Like that of his fellow northerners, his anti-slavery stance grew into abolitionism, his realistic view that the war was fought against secession morphed gradually into a far more idealistic view of a new kind of nation, and then, like so many of them in blue, he was struck down. The nation mourned, and still mourned, as Lincoln became a symbol of the sacrifices to the war he tried to avert. "Scorned and ridiculed by many critics during his presidency, Lincoln became a martyr and almost a saint after his death." He had saved the Union, not singlehandedly, but with single-minded determination.[26]

But did his very representativeness make him great? What great deeds, what shining heroism, did he exhibit? Called the Great Emancipator, he was neither. He genuinely hated slavery. It violated his ideal that a man should benefit from his own labor and that a man should be free to move about seeking work, starting a family, and guiding his children's upbringing. But Lincoln was not in favor of social mixing, and he was a white supremacist. He ended slavery with the Emancipation Proclamation in portions of states still in rebellion, a war powers step that helped recruit blacks into the Union Army and denied their labor to their former owners. He acceded to the Thirteenth Amendment, ending slavery, though it was the work and the idea of others in his party.

Would perhaps a major part of Lincoln's greatness have come to any other man elected to the highest office in these times? Had Lincoln not won the Republican Party nomination in 1860, would we have seen the man as great? Had not the nation been plunged into a Civil War, would his virtues have seemed so evident or his character so luminous? A mental experiment will help us weigh the relative impact of times and the man. The outgoing president, James Buchanan, is reckoned in all the polls one of the worst or the worst of U.S. chief executives. Yet he presided over the same crisis as Lincoln. The times had not changed.

Consider, however, Buchanan's inaugural address, delivered on March 4, 1857:

> In entering upon this great office I must humbly invoke the God of our fathers for wisdom and firmness to execute its high and responsible duties in such a manner as to restore harmony and ancient friendship among the people of the several States and to preserve our free institutions throughout many generations. Convinced that I owe my election to the inherent love for the Constitution and the Union which still animates the hearts of the American people, let me earnestly ask their powerful support in sustaining all just measures calculated to perpetuate these, the richest political blessings which Heaven has ever bestowed upon any nation.

Could these words lift the spirits of a nation? Capture its deepest emotions? Live through the ages?[27]

If Lincoln is great, it is because he is perceived as great, and he is perceived as great because of the enduring power of his words. Historians and lay readers agree on this. An indifferent public speaker with a high-pitched voice, unable to match the dramatic onstage performances of some of his political rivals, Lincoln could out-write them all. As he told the first audience he faced after he announced his candidacy for the U.S. Senate seat held by his great rival Stephen A. Douglas:

If we could first know where we are, and whither we are tending, we could then better judge what to do, and how to do it. . . . A house divided against itself cannot stand. I believe this government cannot endure, permanently half slave and half free. I do not expect the Union to be dissolved—I do not expect the house to fall—but I do expect it will cease to be divided. It will become all one thing or all the other. Either the opponents of slavery will arrest the further spread of it, and place it where the public mind shall rest in the belief that it is in the course of ultimate extinction; or its advocates will push it forward, till it shall become alike lawful in all the States, old as well as new—North as well as South.

The answer was the victory of the free soil Republican Party, a victory that Lincoln foresaw:

Our cause, then, must be intrusted to, and conducted by, its own undoubted friends—those whose hands are free, whose hearts are in the work—who do care for the result. Two years ago [in 1856, the first time the party ran a candidate for the presidency] the Republicans of the nation mustered over thirteen hundred thousand strong. We did this under the single impulse of resistance to a common danger, with every external circumstance against us. Of strange, discordant, and even hostile elements, we gathered from the four winds, and formed and fought the battle through, under the constant hot fire of a disciplined, proud, and pampered enemy. Did we brave all them to falter now?—now, when that same enemy is wavering, dissevered, and belligerent? The result is not doubtful. We shall not fail—if we stand firm, we shall not fail. Wise counsels may accelerate, or mistakes delay it, but, sooner or later, the victory is sure to come.

When the house had divided, President Lincoln told the crowds at his first inaugural, in words that are as moving today as they must have been when so much depended upon them:

My countrymen, one and all, think calmly and well, upon this whole subject. Nothing valuable can be lost by taking time. If there be an object to
hurry any of you, in hot haste, to a step which you would never take delib-
erately, that object will be frustrated by taking time; but no good object
can be frustrated by it. Such of you as are now dissatisfied still have the
old Constitution unimpaired, and, on the sensitive point, the laws of your
own framing under it; while the new administration will have no immediate power, if it would, to change either. If it were admitted that you who
are dissatisfied hold the right side in the dispute, there still is no single
good reason for precipitate action. Intelligence, patriotism, Christianity,
and a firm reliance on Him, who has never yet forsaken this favored land,
are still competent to adjust, in the best way, all our present difficulty. In
your hands, my dissatisfied fellow countrymen, and not in mine, is the
momentous issue of civil war. The government will not assail you. You
can have no conflict without being yourselves the aggressors. You have no
oath registered in Heaven to destroy the government, while I shall have
the most solemn one to "preserve, protect, and defend" it. I am loath to
close. We are not enemies, but friends. We must not be enemies. Though
passion may have strained, it must not break our bonds of affection. The
mystic chords of memory, stretching from every battle-field, and patriot
grave, to every living heart and hearth-stone, all over this broad land, will
yet swell the chorus of the Union, when again touched, as surely they will
be, by the better angels of our nature.

In the midst of a terrible war, surrounded by the graves of so many
young Americans, Lincoln dedicated the Gettysburg, Pennsylvania,
cemetery.

Four score and seven years ago our fathers brought forth on this continent, a new nation, conceived in Liberty, and dedicated to the proposition that all men are created equal. . . . But, in a larger sense, we can not
dedicate—we can not consecrate—we can not hallow—this ground. The

brave men, living and dead, who struggled here, have consecrated it, far above our poor power to add or detract. The world will little note, nor long remember what we say here, but it can never forget what they did here. It is for us the living, rather, to be dedicated here to the unfinished work which they who fought here have thus far so nobly advanced. It is rather for us to be here dedicated to the great task remaining before us—that from these honored dead we take increased devotion to that cause for which they gave the last full measure of devotion—that we here highly resolve that these dead shall not have died in vain—that this nation, under God, shall have a new birth of freedom—and that government of the people, by the people, for the people, shall not perish from the earth.

In a few words, Lincoln encapsulated the republican dream of five generations, and the hope of many more generations to come. As Garry Wills explains, "By giving this language a place in our sacred documents, Lincoln changed the way people thought about the Constitution." The old states' rights idea of a constitution that was a compact among separate entities faded. The Lincoln Constitution was an indissoluble union, a great nation. Equally important, Lincoln taught us how to read the Declaration of Independence. "A single people, dedicated to a proposition" of government for, by, and of all the people, was an "intellectual revolution."[28]

When that war had almost come to a close, Lincoln once again gave an inaugural address, and its serene confidence and magnanimity recapture the dream of a single nation, living in harmony, looking to a better future.

Fondly do we hope—fervently do we pray—that this mighty scourge of war may speedily pass away. Yet, if God wills that it continue, until all the wealth piled by the bond-man's two hundred and fifty years of unrequited toil shall be sunk, and until every drop of blood drawn with the lash, shall be paid by another drawn with the sword, as was said three thousand years ago, so still it must be said "the judgments of the Lord, are true and righteous altogether." With malice toward none; with charity for all; with firmness in the right, as God gives us to see the right, let us strive on to finish the work we are in; to bind up the nation's wounds; to care for him who shall have borne the battle, and for his widow, and his orphan—to do all which may achieve and cherish a just and lasting peace, among ourselves, and with all nations.

His audience listened with intent silence, a profound appreciation for his services, and, most of all, the hope that the peace would bind up the nation. A month and ten days later he lay dying from an assassin's bullet. In 1840, after love seemed to have eluded him once again, he told a friend: "he would have been more than willing to die save that 'he had done nothing to make any human being remember that he had lived.'" Now everyone remembered what he had done, because no one would forget what he had said.[29]

War brings out the hatred in men. Civil war is the worst of wars in this fashion, for both sides feel betrayed by the other. As Wills demonstrates, Lincoln's wartime telegrams to his commanders have an almost brutal sternness and determination. The war must be won at all costs. But Lincoln himself did not hate. Perhaps this was because Mary Todd's brothers—his brothers-in-law—fought for the Confederacy. Perhaps it was because he empathized so easily with the human cost on both sides. Perhaps it was because he hated war itself more than he hated those who would dismember the Union. And perhaps it was because he was always looking beyond the war, confident in victory, to the reknitting of the torn threads of nationhood. His words carried all of these emotions, but not hate.[30]

When C-SPAN issued its early 2009 ranking of the presidents, one of the moderators of the survey said that Lincoln topped the list "because he is perceived to embody the nation's avowed core values: integrity, moderation, persistence in the pursuit of honorable goals, respect for human rights, compassion." Nothing in his life so captured these values as his words. So if greatness is in words—for how else, in the end, would history know who was great—what is the measure, the judgment of greatness of words? Lincoln's words were great because they were enduring, and enduring because they were great—a perfect circle, but one in which all of us live and judge. We know because we know greatness in words like Lincoln's, it strikes us immediately, like poetry we cannot forget or a movie sequence that repeats itself in our heads after we have left the movie house. Greatness cannot be modest. Lincoln was modest in almost all ways, save his gift for language at just the right public moment. He rose to those occasions, as he did not to so many others. It was his vaulting ambition to move hearts and minds with words that so became him, and his time, and ours. It is majestic, sweeping, grand—but not through heavy-handed allusions or flights of fancy. Like Shakespeare's prose, Lincoln's used the commonplaces of language in his time. To be sure, he was part of a tradition of political oratory that included his political forebears like Daniel Webster, Henry Clay, and John C. Calhoun. But who can remember any of their speeches? For they swayed by the tone and drama of their performance, while he swayed not by manner or voice but by words themselves. And because those words were so American—so rooted in deeply held and hotly contested values of freedom and equality—they remain the best markers of Lincoln's continued greatness.[31]

* * *

Because the biographer's judgment of greatness in the last resort depends upon words—stored words, remembered words, words on paper or, now, pixels in the electronic ether—the words of those who have gone before us matter as much as their deeds. For by their words we know them. What would Caesar have been to us without his *Conquest of Gaul*? Or Lincoln if he had been known as "Silent Abe"? Greatness in history is a quality conferred not by life itself but by the pale remnant of life in the historical record. This may been both a facile and cynically logical conclusion. But what biography reminds history is that without sources, there is no history, and without the words of our subjects, we have no history.[32]

It is this dependence on the survival of words that brings history and biography together. How the historians and the biographer read character and motive behind the words may vary, but both students of the past cannot do their work without the words. If the popularity and prize-winning ways of biographies of Lincoln, and his fellows in the pantheon, the founding fathers, are any indication, the "golden age" of biography is not past. It is still with us. If the biographer regards the subject as a hero or a villain, if the biographer over-identifies with the subject, then the biographer forfeits the right to our belief. But by assimilating the methods of the historian proper, by finding objective means to weigh the significance of a life in its times, the biographer's judgment becomes trustworthy.[33]

It is just as important to conclude that the value of the biographer's judgment of greatness does not derive from its finality but from its lack of finality. Just as the historical judgment of one scholar or generation of scholars does not bind the scholar or generation looking at the same documentary evidence, so biographers are free to reassess older judgments of greatness. If one could reply to Ralph Waldo Emerson's epigraph at the start of this chapter, it would be that there is properly no biography; there is only history.

[6]

History and Policy Studies

The tradition and the understanding that you derive from the
lessons of history are among the most important things you
take with you when you graduate.

PRESIDENT HARRY S TRUMAN, graduation address
at the U.S. Naval Academy, May 24, 1952

The study of greatness in men and women often focuses on the decisions
they made—decisions that affected many around them and in some cases
still affect us today. Policy studies, the modern analysis of decision making, has gone far beyond assessments of character and intelligence, the
stuff of most biographies. The story of this companion of history begins
with the creation of the RAND Corporation in 1949, a Research ANd
Development think tank created to study the options for achieving a
lasting peace during the Cold War. RAND mathematicians developed
models for decision making, among which is the so-called Prisoner's
Dilemma. Rational choice theories that RAND churned out became one
source of American strategizing in confronting foreign enemies—in theory replacing old ideas of fear and revenge with far more efficacious ones
of calculated risk avoidance. RAND turned away from history, preferring
the apparently more precise social sciences as guides to decision making,
but invariably and inevitably the policy makers returned to history in a
collaboration that was fruitful on both sides.[1]

RAND was not alone in the effort to predict and manage future events
with greater precision. Modern, post–World War II "policy studies"
spread within the university and think tank world and now straddles

many disciplines in its effort to study the cause and effect of public policies, conflict, and conflict resolution. It is interdisciplinary, empirical,
systematic, and dedicated to the application of information and models to big questions. While many of its concerns are present and future
minded, and many of its practitioners regard academic historians and
their output as irrelevant, policy analysis perforce includes systematic,
goal-oriented historical study of "prior effects" and "past policy performance." Though plagued by an absence of boundaries and a voracious
appetite for theory, it is armed with private and public funding, girded
with expertise, and arrayed in a wide variety of institutional settings. No
study of history's companionate disciplines can ignore policy studies.[2]

Policy makers ask what policy studies can teach them. The essence
of policy studies is understanding the lessons of the past and applying
them to the present and the future. It is this teaching function that makes
policy studies one of history's companions. Not only does historical study
offer lessons, but the capacity of history to tutor present and future generations has long been one of its most potent claims to preeminence in our
culture. As the philosopher and political thinker George Santyana wrote
many years ago, "[T]hose who cannot remember the past are condemned
to repeat it." If the teaching of lessons from the past is the fundamental
purpose of policy studies, history and policy studies are surely the closest
of companions.[3]

War in History and Policy Studies

Managing world conflict has been the central concern of policy studies
since its inception. Indeed, the danger of the Cold War's turning hot
was one reason for government sponsorship of RAND. The military
itself connects war studies to policy studies. There are "War Colleges"
in the military establishment dedicated to the historical study of war.
The U.S. Army War College in Carlisle, Pennsylvania, for example, has
a huge education program for officers and civilians whose purpose is to
explore how past military conflicts can tutor us about the nature of war.

Individual and group problem sets at the War College involve study of history, history lectures, case studies, and gaming and other exercises and often includes civilian historians. So-called strategic culture in these policy analyses weds the historical features of cultures like ours to a study of the "way of war."[4]

The tie between policy studies and war goes further back in history than RAND, the Cold War, and the war colleges. As Harold Lasswell, the father of modern policy studies, wrote, "[I]t should not be supposed that the policy-science orientation is a totally novel idea among scholars." It will come as no surprise that the origin of policy studies was the perceived need to manage warfare. The greatest military strategist of the early modern era, the Prussian officer Carl von Clausewitz, was the first exponent of policy studies. Clausewitz rose from the ranks to a general's place in the Prussian army that participated in the defeat of Napoleon at Waterloo. His musings on war and history were incomplete at his death but have been widely read and quoted since their posthumous publication in 1832—particularly after the spectacular defeat of France's armies by Prussia's in 1870–71. An intellectual in uniform (he was one of the most influential members of the king's staff officers and matured during a time of intellectual ferment in Germany), he stood astride the period of rationalization of war in the eighteenth century ("the military Enlightenment") and the romanticism of war in the nineteenth. He understood that the able organization of the army—its supply, its mobility, its officer corps—was not enough to ensure victory on the field. Modern war (after Napoleon) was far larger in scale than the set piece battles and sieges of the previous years. Precise planning and expert maneuver could never cover all the unexpected consequences of total war. Most important, it was impossible to wage war without political will: thus his most famous aphorism that war was the continuation of diplomacy by other means.[5]

Like the teachers at military academies and the officers on general staffs over the years since his death, modern readers differ whether Clausewitz the realist regarded militarism as a necessary evil, or Clausewitz the amoralist was indifferent to the evils of war. Thus his concept of total war has been read as a command to use any and all means to achieve victory and, contrariwise, as a concession that in war, man's essential animal nature triumphs over his higher self. But there can be no disputing how Clausewitz regarded war's part in history. His dedication to *On War* revealed that the practical advice he offered was the result of his own "continuous study of the history of war. . . . For it is the study of the history of war that has given us these principles." What was this lesson? "War is part of the intercourse of the human race." Military history was the history of mankind. Military history offered countless examples of the principle that "the destruction of the enemy's armed force appears, therefore, always as the superior and more effectual means to which all others must give way." While a state could achieve its aims in war simply by its resolve to fight, battle was still the only sure way to gain victory; indeed, it was the only "moral" way to wage war. Morality lay in victory.[6]

Clausewitz regarded war as a constant of human history, as if the decision to wage war—indeed, every manifestation of human aggression—lay in a realm deeply seated in the human psyche. How did he know this? He read histories. Thus at its very inception policy planning relied upon history, and history's judgment was a sobering one. Perhaps war was rooted in the very nature of men. In 1966, the Nobel Prize–winning zoologist Konrad Lorenz published a troubling book. Lorenz's credentials made the argument of the work—that aggression, and its mass expression in war, was instinctive in homo sapiens—even more disturbing. For not only was he famous for his studies of animal territoriality, he had been an open supporter of the Nazi Party before and during World War II.

In *On Aggression*, Lorenz wrote, "[M]ilitary enthusiasm is a specialized form of communal aggression, clearly distinct from yet functionally related to the more primitive forms of petty individual aggression. . . . Militant enthusiasm in a man is a true autonomous instinct, it has its own appetitive behavior, its own releasing mechanisms, and like the sexual urge or any other strong instinct, it engenders a specific feeling of intense satisfaction." Like the "lower orders" of animals, humans go to war to protect territory, to find mates, and to satisfy our basic needs to dominate.[7]

Historians of war long ago conceded its base nature even as they offered lessons about it. For example, the conquistador–turned–Dominican missionary Bartolomé de las Casas wrote an eyewitness history of the Spanish incursion into the Caribbean island of Hispaniola that reported the conquistadors' almost feral misconduct. "Into this land of meek outcasts there came some Spaniards who immediately behaved like ravening wild beasts, wolves, tigers or lions that had been starved for many days. And Spaniards have behaved in no other way during the past forty years, down to the present time, for they are still acting like ravening beasts, killing, terrorizing, afflicting, torturing, and destroying the native peoples, doing all this with the strangest and most varied new methods of cruelty."[8]

Las Casas described the Indios as victims, and surely after the catastrophic impact of Spanish-borne diseases, pest infestations, and animal depredations on native flora the word "victim" seems appropriate. But it will not do, not as history at least, to idealize the Indians. They raided one another's territory, demanded tribute from their weaker neighbors, enslaved and tortured victims on their own long before the European newcomers brought their own violence to the Americas. When Europeans did arrive, Indian villagers in Florida wiped out a Spanish incursion in 1528 and Indian peoples in the Southeast crippled Hernando De Soto's invasion as it passed through their lands from 1539 to 1542. Indians tortured captives by burning them alive, dismembering them, and in some cases cannibalizing them. The English colonizers called the Cherokee uprising of 1758–61 a "rebellion" and the war loosed by a confederation of Ohio and Great Lakes Indians "Pontiac's Rebellion," but these terms presumed an English sovereignty over the native peoples that never existed. In fact there were outbreaks of a war between Americans and Europeans in South America, Central America, North America, and the Caribbean that began in 1492 and did not end until the last Ghost Dancer at Wounded Knee was slaughtered.

Las Casas convinced King Philip II of Spain to offer his protection to the Indios, but at the same time the demand for labor in the sugar plantations of the Spanish and Portuguese New World empires promoted the transatlantic slave trade. The lessons of violence paled before the prospect of riches. Many of the Africans brutally jammed into the slave ships like sardines in a tin had been the losers in Africa's endemic and endless wars. Others were kidnaped from the coast or taken from villages inland. Indeed, the profitability of the slave trade to its African partners triggered more wars to obtain more slaves. Technological achievement led not to peace but to more effectively waged wars.

A neutral observer of the expansion of Europe after 1600 might well conclude that "the first payoff of the industrial revolution would be spent on arms and armies. . . . Major European wars were partly fought in places as distant from centers of [European] power as Pondicherry or Pittsburgh." The more civilized we have become, the more our ability to make war on "the other" has spread and the more war one finds in the historical record. Andrew Jackson's personal campaign (he lacked sanction from the administration in Washington for it) against the Creeks and Seminole people included hanging prisoners. To be sure, his men were appalled by the scalps of their former neighbors they found on poles in the warring Creeks' villages. The Mexican-American War began with exchanges of flags of truce and other military courtesies but by its second year had descended into atrocities so common that even the pro-war newspapers reported "deeds of wanton violence and cruelty." The Sepoy Wars in the Anglo-Indian Raj of the 1850s, the first stage of the suppression of guerrilla warfare in the Philippines, the Rif War in Spanish Morocco in the 1920s, the wars for Vietnamese independence against the French in the 1950s—all left scenes of horror in their wake. One could multiply these examples by the hundreds. From 1990 to 2008 there have been more than 120 wars around the world. In 2012, the United Nations Security Council debated how many civilians had to be slaughtered by their own government in Syria before the carnage could be officially termed a "civil war." The Cold War is over and the great powers are at peace with one another, but more than 100 of these conflicts are civil wars and almost all have an ethnic or tribal component. The victims are largely noncombatants, and there seem to be no rules except revenge and kill or be killed. Why did militias massacre women in children in Rwanda? For the same reason that militias murdered women and children during the civil wars in Lebanon, Sri Lanka, the Congo, Bosnia, and Chechnya. There is nothing heroic or virtuous in these wars. Indeed, there are almost no words to describe them.[9]

But we try, for an objective view of history cannot omit war, so pervasive has it been throughout the world's past. And the study of war has lessons to offer. Some of these seem perverse, for the progress of war goes hand-in-hand with the progress of technologies, from stone defenses, to iron armor, to firearms, and apace with the progress of better ideas for defense and attack. The modern city owes its landscape to seventeenth-century French military architecture, for example, and the modern encyclopedia owes itself to Maurice of Nassau's printed manual of arms. As John Keegan, the dean of modern military historians, has written, "History reminds us that the states in which we live, their institutions, even their laws, have come to us through conflict, often of the most bloodthirsty sort."[10]

It may even be argued that the first purpose of history was to record the deeds of warriors and the struggles of one people against another. Certainly, the earliest histories that have come down to us are stories of war. To modern eyes, they seem a mix of fancy and fact. Who regards *The Iliad*, for example, as a history, yet it certainly recalls a very real conflict between Mycenaean Greeks and the Hittite tributary Troy. The ancient Greek historian Herodotus wrote to explain the reasons for the Persian invasion of Greece. Two generations later, Thucydides' history aimed to explain the Peloponnesian War between Athens and Sparta. Julius Caesar's *The Conquest of Gaul* related the Roman invasion of its northern neighbor. Mayan hieroglyphs narrated rounds of combat among Mayan city-states. The Heike Monogatari recalled the bitter clan warfare of the Taira and the Minamoto clans, a civil war that rocked Japan in the last years of the twelfth century and was told, like *The Iliad*, over evening entertainment by the descendants of the victorious clans. Both Sioux and Crow storytellers retell their two hundred years of conflict, part of a story of endemic raiding on the eastern edges of the great plains.[11]

Even for the military historian who pretends to objectivity, the need to justify victory shapes any discussion of violence. For example, nineteenth-century historians of the American West like Theodore Roosevelt regarded the wars that cleared the land of Native Americans and opened the way for European settlement as a positive good. It was simply the Indians' fate to give way. As he wrote not long after the wars had ended, "It was impossible long to keep peace on the border between the ever encroaching whites and their fickle and blood-thirsty foes. The hard, reckless, often brutalized frontiersmen" faced "Indians as treacherous as they were ferocious." But civilization had to triumph over primitive savagery. Roosevelt's attitude was typical of his generation. David Stannard, a modern historian, recounts that after one brutal encounter between settlers and plains Indians, a gathering of the well-to-do at the Denver Opera House agreed that it would be best to exterminate all the Indians.[12]

Just War and Holy War

For some students of policy, the lessons of war itself can be justified by renaming the atavistic urge to conquer and subdue, and some historians have bowed to these conventions. The concept of a "just war" has a history tied to the honor of warriors in battle and the humane treatment of noncombatants. Greek warriors in *The Iliad* fought Trojan warriors according to a code that both sides accepted, at least according to Homer, the Greek source of information on the war. Even the gods on Olympus understood the code. Athena, seeing the Greeks flee, supposedly said to her brother Apollo, "But to make either army cease, what order shall be given?" He replied, "We will direct the spirit that burns in Hector's breast, to challenge any Greek to wounds, with single powers impressed, which Greeks (admiring) will accept, and make someone stand out, so stout a challenge to receive with a defense as stout." The Romans stood at the edge of enemy territory and declared their grievances aloud. Presumably this prepared the enemy for the onslaught. In fact, the Romans gave potential enemies plenty of notice; the rituals of announcing the imminent war were the last and least parts of ritual.[13]

The foremost Christian commentators on the rules of a just war were Saint Augustine and Saint Thomas Aquinas. Augustine, who as bishop of Hippo in North Africa had seen his share of warfare, explained that a just war could not be a matter of private vengeance. It must be declared by a ruler; it must have a genuine cause; and it must be waged justly. Intention mattered. "True religion looks upon as peaceful those wars that are waged not for motives of aggrandizement, or cruelty, but with the object of securing peace, of punishing evil-doers, and of uplifting the good." Aquinas discussed the just war in his *Summa Theologica*. War should be a last resort, and a just ruler should not initiate war except in extreme circumstances, for example to protect his lands or his people. The target of the war must be limited to those who pose the danger, and the means of prosecuting the war must be appropriate to its object. These strictures were necessary to prevent war from igniting the violent instincts of men, who might otherwise lose all control in war and slaughter the innocents.[14]

To be sure, there were ways for Christian warriors to have their just war in an unjust fashion. No one was more legalistic in claiming lands than the Spanish in America. The native often objected to the Spanish claims of sovereignty, but the Spanish had an answer—the just war. The eminent historian John Elliott explains how that answer worked: "Since a favorable reaction of the indigenous population to such a take-over could hardly be taken for granted, their willingness to submit peacefully came to be tested by the formal reading aloud to them of the *requerimiento*." Crafted in 1512 by a Spanish jurist specifically for this occasion, the document, "after briefly outlining Christian doctrine and the history of the human race, explained that Saint Peter and his successors possessed jurisdiction over the whole world, and had granted the newly discovered lands to Ferdinand and Isabella and their heirs, to whom the local population had to submit, or face the waging of a just war against them." Even assuming the natives' desire for peace, the document itself was read aloud in a language they could not understand—hardly a just way to begin a conquest.[15]

The Nuremburg Laws of 1935 in Nazi Germany were another example of the *requerimiento*, a legal basis for an unjust "just war." Germany under Hitler had one of the most well-developed juristic systems in the world. A combination of traditional Germanic law, Roman law, statutory enactment, and learned commentary, the German legal system was a model of modernity. But definition and debasement of people of Jewish ancestry as a despised racial minority was both historically and ethically flawed. Anyone with a Jewish grandparent was stripped of citizenship and subjected to discriminatory treatment. Jews became the scapegoat for every real and imagined disability Germany faced. The road from the Nuremburg Laws to the death camps was not yet paved, but the camps followed soon upon the Laws, part of a war against one segment of German (and later European) population according to explicit government policy. It was a war of extermination whose aim was a Jew-free Europe. Six million Jews died as a direct result. "It was impossible not to know the Jews' fate. Soldiers and officers wrote home of mass shootings (one letter explicitly details the massacre of 30,000 Jews in a single town), and when they returned on leave, they spoke of the murders in private and in public."[16]

The "just war" is thus a justification for war, part of history, not some extra-historical, natural law category. Justifications follow perceptions of national interest, national honor, national security, and a list of *casus belli* that go back to the first compilations of "the law of nations" in sixteenth-century Spain. But the historical record of war is not without its ironic twist, for as the means of waging atomic, chemical, and biological warfare have become more terrifying, the formal rules of war have become far more humane. They are embodied in the so-called Hague and Geneva conventions, based on rules drafted in 1863 by Francis Lieber (at Lincoln's instigation), with amendments continuing to this day. For example, the provisions for captured soldiers require that they be allowed to keep personal possessions, that they be removed from active combat zones as soon as possible, that they be housed and fed according to the same standards as the captors' own soldiers, that they be treated according to their rank, that they not be forced to work on war-related projects, that they not be tortured for information, and that they be allowed to send mail (subject to censorship) and receive mail and packages (subject to search).[17]

A different set of policy assumptions led even earlier planners to define and wage "holy war" and historians to justify it. The holy war is a war fought against palpable evil. It may be aggressive, for example the many crusades launched by Catholic forces against the Muslim occupiers of Jerusalem, or the Jihad, by which Islam spread over the Mediterranean world. Because the war is undertaken for religious rather than purely secular reasons, its objective was the conversion of the subject popula- tion. Limits on the conduct of soldiers in just wars did not apply to holy wars, for God gave victory, and God had turned His face away from the defeated. Thus religious wars to extirpate or convert the heathen and punish the infidel are among the most savage in human history.

Let us now bring our long aside on the lessons of just and holy war back to the connection between policy studies and historical knowledge. Michael Walzer, a political scientist and policy studies expert, has spent a good deal of time thinking about the old ideas of the just war and the holy war. He connected these with Clausewitz's notion that war was sim- ply a matter of calculation. "In this way, the belligerent is again driven to adopt a middle course. He would act on the principle of using no greater force, and setting himself no greater military aim, than would be sufficient for the achievement of his political aim." Psychological warfare, for example, so long as it was in measured proportion to the political war aims, was permissible—no moral penumbras, no second thoughts. War waged for these goals meant never having to say you were sorry. Surely, if one is realistic, one has to concede that wars are fought for territorial advantage, revenge, to obtain raw materials or laborers, or to strike fear into adversaries who may not even be on the field of battle.[18]

But even the most cynical of realists among policy planners must con- cede the difference between a war fought without rules and a war fought under rules. These rules have evolved over centuries and prescribe the treatment of the wounded enemy, the enemy prisoner, civilian populations, and neutrals. Those who break the rules are war criminals. Violence is thus contained if not wholly constrained—a thought that brought Walzer back to the war crimes trials after World War II. For the victorious Allies claimed that the Axis leaders had broken the rules of war and must pay for their conduct. They were tried and they were punished. Was World War II a just war as waged by the Allies, then, insofar as its conclusion underscored the premise of the just war? In part, the answer depends upon the judge's perspective. For although the laws of war are prescriptive, any historical account of the conduct of war is descriptive— and thus subject, like biography, to the perspective of the historian.

   When one combatant has violated the rules of a just war, its enemy may consider itself similarly licensed to turn from just war to holy war. Historical lessons are replete with cases of this type. The Japanese violated the tenets of the just war by attacking Pearl Harbor without formal warning, though in fact Japanese diplomats in Washington were instructed to deliver such a declaration to Secretary of State Cordell Hull minutes before the attack was to begin. (They were still decoding the encrypted instructions when the first Japanese bombers arrived over Hawaii.) The Japanese treatment of prisoners of war and occupied countries' civilians violated the rules of war. In Japan's defense, it may be argued that the Japanese had never ratified the Geneva or the Hague conventions mandating such conduct, but not that fact notwithstanding, Japan's conduct of the Pacific War induced in part the Allies' decision to strike at population centers in Japan.

A Good War?

Can a switch from historical narrative to a policy studies approach to hostilities add a vital element to the collaboration between history and policy studies? Can it teach lessons that save us from the uncertain and subjective impact of wars entered or waged for the wrong reasons? A new set of questions is impelled by this shift in viewpoint. How are the students of war policy to judge any particular war? How might the planner and the historian engage in a conversation about their differing ways of rendering judgment? Consider two examples, World War II and the Iraq War, in light of questions a policy planning/history perspective raises.

Casualties in World War II totaled more than 70 million soldiers, sailors, airmen, and civilians. The former Soviet Union leads in this category, with more than 25 million dead. China, whose long war with Japan began in 1937, follows with 20 million dead. Germany had more than 7 million, but unlike those of the USSR and China, Germany's dead were overwhelmingly men in arms (more than 5 million). Japan as well had nearly 3 million dead, but 80 percent of these were men in uniform. The United Kingdom and the United States lost a little under 500,000 and 450,000 dead, respectively, but most were uniformed soldiers, sailors, and airmen. The German air campaign over Britain cost the British nearly 70,000 civilian lives. While not as deadly as the great plagues of the fourteenth century, World War II left its fatal mark on more than fifty nations.[19]

Advocates of the good war thesis argue that violence can be condoned in the name of the defeat of evil. Certainly stark choices between good and evil present themselves to those who lead in war. This was true of President Franklin D. Roosevelt on the eve of U.S. entry into the war. Despite his "hesitations and evasions, his wary deference to the isolationists, and his frequently cagey misrepresentations to the American public," he believed that the Axis powers were evil. Domestic politics, including his own party's platform, dictated that he not to go to war until war was thrust upon him. He understood the dangers of letting the Axis powers win, but equally important he understood that America was not fully ready for war. The country was already the arsenal of democracy by 1941 but was psychologically unprepared for the sacrifices of war. The day of infamy, December 7, 1941, with the unannounced Japanese attack on the naval base at Pearl Harbor, followed by the German declaration of war four days later, gave the United States the moral high ground to enter the war.[20]

Once committed, America mobilized for total war but conducted itself under the rules of a just war. Or so it was said. Captured enemy combatants and civilians in occupied areas were treated in accord with the Geneva and Hague conventions. But the United States did not hesitate to use conventional weapons against civilian targets. The daylight bombing campaign against Germany may have claimed to pinpoint military targets and avoid civilian population, but the firebomb attacks on Tokyo had the explicit opposite aim. General Curtis LeMay, commander of American air forces in the Pacific, "deployed two intimidating new technologies against Japan's highly inflammable cities, where most people lived in wooden homes. The first was a fiendishly efficient six-pound incendiary bomblet . . . which spewed burning gelatinized gasoline that stuck to its targets and was virtually inextinguishable by conventional means." The results of the carpet bombing of Tokyo with these weapons in the late winter of 1945 were "concentric rings that soon merged into a sea of flame. . . . When the raiders flew away, shortly before four A.M.[,] they left behind them one million homeless Japanese and nearly ninety thousand dead. The victims died from fire, asphyxiation, and falling buildings. Some boiled to death in superheated canals and ponds where they had sought refuge from the flames." LeMay saw what he had done and called it good. Until the end of the war, his bombers attacked sixty-six more times, reducing much of Japan's urban areas to ash. Nearly one million Japanese died in the firebombing offensive, and many more were injured. In this holocaust, the atomic bombing of Hiroshima and Nagasaki, largely civilian targets left for last, seemed a fittingly horrific climax.[21]

Statements of high purpose could not prevent the violence of war from etching itself upon the hearts of those who waged it. For "the greatest generation," the sobriquet that the journalist Tom Brokaw used to describe the veterans of World War II, "the horrors of war gave birth to a new generation of good Samaritans. Young men and women who have been so intensely exposed to such inhumanity make a silent pledge that if ever they escape this dark world of death and injuries, this universe of cruelty, they will devote their lives to good works." But others lived in a perpetually dark world after the war, even if they did not suffer catastrophic physical injuries. For the psychological effect of combat is itself devastating. Now it is called postcombat stress disorder. In World War II it was called battle fatigue. When first diagnosed, in World War I, it was called shell shock. The symptoms remain remarkably similar: inability to sleep, irritability, shifts in mood, lethargy or unexplained inability to complete tasks, various otherwise undiagnosable muscle pains and lack of mobility, and, worst of all, a sense of shame, guilt, or suicidal impulses. As Brigadier General Gary S. Patton explained after he returned from service in the Iraq War, "I've had sleep interruptions from loud noises. Of course there's no [improvised explosive devices] or rockets going off in my bedroom, but the brain has a funny way of remembering those things, not only recreating the exact sound, but also the smell of the battlefield and the metallic taste you get in your mouth when you have that same incident on the battlefield." In some cases, the patient becomes suicidal or homicidal.[22]

Perhaps the individual outcomes suitable for historical study are not as suitable for policy study pronouncements. The latter bid us fly higher over the terrain of battle. Policy study welcomes blue-sky hypotheticals. Would the world have been better if Germany had been unopposed in its demand for Danzig and the Polish Corridor? Or if England and France had not declared war when Germany invaded Poland? Certainly Italy did not benefit from joining the Axis powers in 1940, and Japan did not benefit from its attack on the United States. The results of the war were certainly not beneficial for Nazi Germany, fascist Italy, or imperial Japan, but what about the Soviet Union? At the time of what was portrayed as the Great Patriotic War, in fact the Russians were remarkably unprepared and nearly overwhelmed when the Nazis invaded. China's woes continued long after the war with a civil war between Communist and Nationalist forces. The United States emerged as the winner and in combination of generosity and shrewd calculation helped both its allies and the former Axis countries rebuild under the so-called Marshall Plan.

Again, adopting a policy studies point of view, can one judge the war not from any single nation's standpoint but from the overall results? The direct results were the toppling of three dictatorships and the imposition of Soviet puppet governments in much of eastern Europe. The Cold War between the newly expanded Soviet Bloc and the Western powers was a direct result of the removal of the German buffer. The Cold War spread to Africa and Asia as European empires in those continents were dismantled. With the nuclear threat on both sides, the Cold War posed a danger of world annihilation that World War II did not pose.

Another direct result of the war's end was the emergence of the United States as the world's greatest superpower. This imposed global responsibilities on the country that its prewar policy of isolation did not. The United States was to be peacekeeper, aider, and comforter of the weak and stern alternative to Communism, mutually exclusive roles. The result was a series of wars in Asia, including the Korean and Vietnam wars. Plainly, the good war may have unexpected and dire consequences.

A Bad War?

The causes, progress, and significance of the Iraq War of 2003–10 are still hot-button issues for policy planners because in many ways, it was their war. Policy experts in the government and academia offered their services to civilian and military planners throughout the war. Although the events are still recent at this writing, historical scholars have already offered thoughts on the invasion that future planners may adopt, for some of that commentary reflects poorly on prewar and wartime policy. With one eye on the Iraq War, and one eye on the next war, the historian bids the policy planner think hard about the temporal context for the war.

In other words, history bids policy students ask contextual questions, questions that frame the Iraq War in historical terms. While there is a great deal more for historians of the war to study, one already can use it as a template for the interaction of history and policy planning. A first set of questions that historians would want policy planners to consider entails the origin of the war. Did it begin with Britain's creation of the modern state of Iraq at the end of World War I; with the struggle between Allied and Axis power for Iraq during World War II; with the rise of the Ba'ath Party and Saddam Hussein to power during the Cold War; with Operation Desert Storm, the multinational effort to drive Iraq forces from Kuwait; or with Operation Iraqi Freedom itself? The point of questions like these is to deepen the connection between history and policy studies and to make policy studies more effective. There will likely be more wars in which policy planners play a role, and if the Iraq War offers any lesson, it is that effective policy must take account of history.[23]

A different set of questions the historian can pose to the planner concern subject matter: Is the Iraq War a purely military operation? The old aphorism about generals fighting the next war with the lessons of the previous one is apposite to the Iraq War. Horrific casualties in the American Civil War were the product of offensive tactics that had worked in the Mexican-American War but were outmoded by the new technologies of 1861–65. The trench warfare lessons of World War I ill prepared the French to counter the German Blitzkrieg (lighting war) of 1940. The lessons of the French forces combating Ho Chi Minh in Vietnam were misapplied by the United States during the Vietnam War. Massive troop build-ups did not secure the borders of South Vietnam against North Vietnamese incursions. History teaches that even highly successful military operations will fail to fulfill their political purposes if policy planners do not have a clear plan for the reconstruction of defeated enemies. As Americans in Iraq became garrison troops surrounded by warring clans, religious sects, and political parties, postwar casualties exceeded those of the invasion. In no way did they rival Vietnam (more than 50,000 dead versus fewer than 5,000), but the postwar psychological problems of the veterans, the thousands of catastrophic wounds, the cost of the war in the hundreds of billions of dollars, and the massive disillusion on the home front with the war showed that Vietnam's lessons had not been learned by those who planned the Iraq invasion. In short, the military and political planners were looking at the wrong war—Desert Storm instead of Vietnam—for guidance.[24]

Perhaps the proper subject matter for study was not military at all, but political and diplomatic. The Iraq War was launched as part of a war on terrorists and their supporters. The argument President George W. Bush proffered was that Iraqi dictator Saddam Hussein had stocks of chemical and biological, perhaps even nuclear, weapons or material to make weapons which he could and would provide to anti-American terrorists. In the wake of the attacks of September 11, 2001, the fear of even wider and more deadly terrorist attacks on U.S. soil seemed warranted. In fact, the 9/11 suicide attackers were not Iraqis but were Saudis and Egyptians (our nominal allies); Hussein did not have stockpiles of weapons of mass destruction; and Hussein's regime was, as much as any in the Middle East, the enemy of the Islamic fundamentalism that fed terrorist manpower. American intelligence and strategic planning were far off base in targeting Hussein.

Conspiracy theorists posited another reason for the Bush invasion of Iraq. Hussein and Bush's father, former President George H.W. Bush, were deadly personal antagonists. The war thus had the semblance of a family feud. Certainly family ties were part of American diplomatic relationships with Saudi Arabia, Hussein's ultimate target when he ordered his troops into Kuwait in 1990. Equally important from a diplomatic standpoint, Hussein was hated within his own country by the majority Shi'a (he was a Sunni, the majority of Middle Eastern Muslims, but not the majority in Iraq), by the Kurds whose villages he had systematically destroyed, and by the Iranians, whose country he had invaded in 1980. If the purpose of the war was not to protect Americans from terrorists (for the war and its aftermath claimed more American dead than the 9/11 attacks) but to spread democracy, then its lessons would be different from the military ones.

Conjectures may be part of lessons for policy planners, but not for historians. Conjecture may, if properly posed, provide alternatives to what happened, allowing speculation about the consequences of unselected options. Historians are not as enamored of conjecture but are not opposed to hypotheticals when they illuminate the analysis of what did, in fact, occur. What if the Bush administration, having been satisfied that there were no weapons of mass destruction in Iraq, and that Hussein had no connection to Al Qaeda or any other terrorist organization, had declared a diplomatic triumph without resort to arms? Would terrorism throughout the world have declined? Given that Iraq was not a major source of terrorist activities to begin with, the answer is a qualified no. On the other hand, did the invasion and the occupation increase terrorist activity? Although terror groups did try to leverage the war into a recruiting device, that does not seem to have increased terrorism. The attacks on allied forces in Iraq were not the work of terrorists. Sometimes called insurrectionists, sometimes given other names, those who committed violence against allied forces and civilians friendly to the allied mission are largely derived from Iraqi politics. The weapons, including the improvised anti-personnel devices, are of native design or have come from the regular governments of Syria and Iran, not from terrorist organizations.

A realist approach, the essence of policy studies, would ask what were the costs and gains, assuming that war is a kind of game (as in a RAND study) in which the winner's costs are lower than its gains. Joseph Stiglitz and Linda Bilmes have attempted to total and examine the "tradeoff" of these costs and gains in the Iraq War. They argued that the volunteer army's costs in death and debility (some 4,000 dead and more than 25,000 wounded) hid the true human cost because the callup was not based on a draft. The financial costs of the war, in the hundreds of billions of dollars, was hidden by borrowing the money rather than raising a tax to pay for it or issuing war bonds. The all-volunteer army is composed of professionals and enlistees, the former whose occupation is war, the latter from the silent lower classes. In addition, much of the garrison duty was subcontracted to private companies like Blackwater. The total cost of the war will exceed $2 trillion, including interest on the borrowing. The most obvious sign of the concealment of the deaths of members of the armed forces was the ban on media coverage of the returning coffins. The most obvious sign of the debilitating financial burden is the upwardly spiraling national debt. Add to this the cost in human life and property to the Iraqis, and the balance sheet is surely weighted in favor of loss.[25]

When policy planners and historians put their heads together in the future (as they should have in 2003) they will very likely see the Iraq adventure in a different light from that cast by politicians ready to engage in war at the time. Such a history might teach that "modern" Iraq—its cities, its infrastructure, its formal political parties and institutions—is only "skin deep." Iraq in 2003 remained what it had always been, a congeries of tribes, sects, clans, families, and localities. In short, it was not a nation and could not be treated as such. Thus, even if the war itself was easily winnable, and it was, and Saddam Hussein and the Ba'ath Party were easily toppled, and they were, the democratization and modernization of Iraq by a foreign power would be almost impossible. Divisions within the Sunni and Shi'a, divisions within the Kurdish parties, personal rivalries, and the incapacity of government to provide the most basic public services would (and did) undermine the occupation. Little civil wars, really wars within neighborhoods, partitioned the cities and the countryside into ethnic and sectarian enclaves. The United States had broken it and now had to buy it.[26]

If history is any guide, Iraq will not be the United States' last theater of war. The Afghan War preceded the conflict in Iraqi and has already outlived it. When Allied troops withdraw, the same tribal system that preceded the occupation will reassert itself. Despite the failure of U.S. military policy in Vietnam, the cost, the swelling domestic opposition, and the political fallout, the next generation of military and political leaders of the United States readily deployed military forces around the world, in Panama, Grenada, Lebanon, Kuwait, Afghanistan, and Iraq. The late Senator George S. McGovern of South Dakota is reputed to have said, as he campaigned to end the Vietnam War, that "at least we'll never have to go down that road again." He was wrong. The lessons of Vietnam did not deter the government from engaging in military activities in foreign lands. Nor will the lessons of Iraq, or of Afghanistan.[27]

To be sure, there will no doubt be adjustments in future military and diplomatic tactics as a result of the Iraq experience. This is true of every war. These may include greater use of mercenaries, fuller consultation with allies, more planning for postwar reconstruction, and greater reliance on technology and intelligence gathering. None of these changes will deter the United States or any other nation from entering another war for perceived ideological or economic or strategic advantage, or to protect the national interest, or to preserve national security. At home, the unprecedented use of executive authority to imprison suspected terrorists and invade the privacy of suspected terrorist sympathizers during the administration of George W. Bush, and at his behest, may be rolled back. But as there were precedents for the domestic intelligence gathering initiative during his administration in the administrations of Abraham Lincoln, Woodrow Wilson, Harry S Truman, and Richard M. Nixon, so future administrations, citing national security needs, may set aside constitutional protections of individual rights. For the Iraq War is a tragedy, a story of a great nation's falling because of its hubris. History and its lessons did not matter. The planners would create their "own reality." It is a lesson that fills the history books.[28]

Policy planners may conclude that violence is amoral, war is inevitable, and in wartime purveyors of historical judgment must stand aside. What is amoral is beyond good and evil. It may be justified or justifiable. It may be necessary or unavoidable. But the consequences of unceasing war cannot be so easily dismissed, even by the most clear-eyed policy planner. For endless war ruined entire civilizations, like the Mayan. It destroyed empires, like the Spanish. It wasted resources and dislocated populations. It killed and maimed the young and the old who did not bear arms. So war may doom our "great experiment" in liberty.

Here the generalities of policy studies should bow to the particulars of historical recollection. No Union general contributed more to the defeat of the Confederacy than William T. Sherman. An innovator in the concept of total war, including the destruction of the southern homefront (though his soldiers were ordered not to harm civilians unless attacked),

Sherman wrote at the end of the war, "I confess, without shame, that I am sick and tired of fighting—its glory is all moonshine; even success the most brilliant is over dead and mangled bodies, with the anguish and lamentations of distant families, appealing to me for sons, husbands, and fathers. . . . [I]t is only those who have never heard a shot, never heard the shriek and groans of the wounded and lacerated . . . that cry aloud for more blood, more vengeance, more desolation." Even in the "good war"—World War II—the sentiments of the combat soldiers and officers separated the purpose of the war from its reality. As Gene La Rocque, later an admiral in the U.S. Navy, told Studs Terkel, an oral historian and radio personality, "In that four years [of war in the Pacific] I thought, what a hell of a waste of a man's life. I lost a lot of friends. . . . I stayed in the navy because I believed the United States could really make the world safe for democracy. I went around to high schools in uniform, telling the kids I thought war was stupid, to ignore all this baloney that shows up in poetry and novels and movies about gallantry and heroism and beauty. I told them it's just a miserable, ugly business." Larocque worried that "World War II has warped our view of how we look at things today. We see things in terms of that war, which in a sense was a good war. But the twisted memory of it encourages men of my generation to be willing, almost eager, to use military force anywhere in the world." The admiral spoke not as a military commander, a hierarch in a hierarchy, but as one of the millions of Americans who went to war.[29]

The Lessons of History

The historians have never fully ceded the field of policy studies to the policy planners. The historians want, and because of the very nature of historical inquiry they will have, the last words. In a fashion characteristic of the way that historians borrowed and absorbed the tenets of other disciplines, historians have taken policy studies to heart. The results are histories that ask sobering and instructive policy studies–like questions about war and peace in the modern world.

Two of the most celebrated and probing of these inquisitors are Paul Kennedy and Niall Ferguson. They are exemplars of policy-infused historical writing. Kennedy's much-read and -discussed *The Rise and Fall of the Great Powers* (1987) posed a rule for the dominant world power at any time in its supremacy: Any number-one nation or empire had to "preserve a balance" between military expenditures and its national product, and it had to maintain the foundations of its economic wealth. No nation had.[30]

Kennedy surveyed the great powers from the pre-industrial period through the end of the twentieth century and discovered that over and over they had declined and fell because they let expenditure outrun the means to finance their supremacy, resulting in the erosion of the economic base. It was true of the Spanish Empire, the English Empire, and the Soviet Union, and he predicted that it would become true of the United States. "The argument in this book is that there exists a dynamic for change, driven chiefly by economic and technological developments, which then impacts upon social structures, political systems, military power, and the position of individual states and empires. . . . Because of man's innate drive to improve his position, the world has never stood still. . . . As some areas of the world have risen, others have fallen behind." Economic conditions enabled and disenabled the rise and fall of nations and empires. Those that overreached created the conditions of their own decline. Kennedy warned that the United States had come close to "imperial overstretch" because of its skyrocketing national debt—and this in 1987! From the vantage point of the second decade of the twenty-first century, it appears that his prediction has more than a little validity.[31]

Ferguson viewed the larger lessons of Western history in a somewhat different light. Kennedy is a military historian viewing empire through an economic lens. Ferguson is an economic historian viewing empire through a cultural lens. Kennedy threw his net widely. Ferguson focused on the Anglophone empires, British and American. Kennedy viewed empire with a critical eye in the cyclical theory of big lessons. Ferguson liked empire, believing that it brings good things to bad places in linear fashion. For him, imperial dominion was natural, based on military and economic power, and if the purpose of empire was extraction of the raw materials of the colony, in return the Anglophone imperial powers brought the dream of a better life.

The British sent missionaries, doctors, and lawgivers to their colonies, along with "British values" of learning, freedom, and national pride. The Americans brought health standards, local capitalism, free markets, self-determination, and democracy. The "colossus" of American power at the beginning of the twenty-first century faced a critical question. During the administration of President Bill Clinton, "the leaders of the one state with the economic resources to make the world a better place . . . to depose these tyrants and impose democratic government . . . lacks the guts to do it." Under the administration of President George W. Bush, the United States had opted to play the role assigned it by history, the liberal empire, but still needed the will to see itself in that role. History taught that "Americans should recognize the functional resemblance between the Anglophone power present and past, and should try to do a better rather than a worse job of policing an unruly world than their British predecessors. In learning from the history of other empires, American will learn not arrogance but precisely that humility which, as a candidate for the presidency, George W. Bush once recommended to his countrymen." From the vantage point of the twenty-first century, Ferguson's lesson looks somewhat dubious.[32]

My point is not that Kennedy was right and Ferguson wrong, and certainly not that either is a better historian than the other, for they are both excellent, but that all lessons, including those as opposite one another as Kennedy's and Ferguson's, return to the questions that policy makers want answered. They are histories written to be applied to the world by those who shape it. Learned historical syntheses of high diplomacy, grand strategy, and the role of leadership of this kind show that the tradition of analytical historical writing born in the classical world and nurtured by the rise of modern nation states is alive and well.

* * *

The choice of policy, the conclusion one reaches from reading the two scholars, remains the reader's. That is to say, if to some readers Kennedy's cyclical theory better fits the past than Ferguson's linear theory, it is because the reader is pessimistic about the future. If Ferguson's seems to fit, it is because the reader is optimistic. In short, the lesson one finds more compelling depends upon one's own outlook, hardly a reassuring conclusion about the contribution of history to policy making or history to policy study. A more reassuring conclusion from the foregoing is that Kennedy and Ferguson have given us much to ponder, and if the choice of what to believe is still ours, it is now a far better informed choice.

Policy planning is a valuable tool, but not a standalone tool. It requires mature historical scholarship to pass its own judgments and is in turn the kind of secondary source that mature historians will find useful. Were it to incorporate not only the findings of historians but something of care of historical method, policy studies would be a trustworthy companion of history. While historians may be blind, or wear blinders, to their own prejudices and allegiances, in the end it is wise and balanced historical study that enables us to understand great events like war and, one hopes, peace.

[7]

History and the Law

We cannot understand a political system . . . and its
laws . . . without a knowledge of the people who have adopted
it . . . for nothing is more evident, than what will conduct one
people to ruin, may lead another, which has a different history and training . . . on the high road to national greatness
and prosperity.

THOMAS M. COOLEY, "Some Considerations
Regarding the Study of the Law" (1884)

The cartoonist and wit Jimmy Hatlo's "There Oughta Be a Law" was
a long-running newspaper feature. He solicited topics for the cartoon
from his readers. Their responses captured an essential fact about law in
America. Americans are a people of laws. We have always expected the
law to express our values. We have certainly made a lot of law, and we
are surrounded by constitutions, acts of Congress, state statutes, court
rulings, executive decrees, and municipal ordinances. We have more lawyers and more litigation than any modern society, and our passion for
going to law, following cases in the media, and debating over laws about
to be and already passed amounts to a national pastime. Our past reveals
law that "has crawled crabwise over the landscape of our history, pulled
and driven by competing notions of rights and duties. The result is not a
single path of the law, but a multiplicity of paths, some deeply trodden,
others ending abruptly, going nowhere."[1]

One cannot study law without seeing its close ties to history. Jurisprudence, the science of law, teaches that law is the command of the state that one

disregards at one's peril, but also that law is as well the reflection of a people's values. Both of these turn the student of law's attention to history. The documentary record of the command of the state is part of its political history. The values of the people are the living tissue of its social and cultural past.

In the Anglo-American "common law system," law and history are technically bound. Unlike "code" systems based on Roman law, the common law's highest authority was the decisions of its appeals courts. The opinions of the justices in these courts, explaining why they decided a case as they did, in effect provided a documentary, historical record of the law to which later courts could refer as they decided appeals. "Precedent," as it was called, was inherently historical because of both its documentary nature and the way in which past decisions came alive again each time they were cited in new cases. This is called *stare decisis*, and it means that courts should be bound by precedent. Precedent—and with it history—has an authority inherent in common law. "The past is supposed to govern the present."[2]

Thomas M. Cooley, perhaps the greatest legal scholar of the Reconstruction Era of American history, understood this close tie between law and history. In lectures he prepared for his classes at the University of Michigan Law School and published as *Principles of the Constitution* (1880), he proposed that law and history were inseparable. Though the lessons of history could be "painful," they were not to be ignored by those who framed the laws. Were any jurisprudent to have a better claim to preeminence than Cooley, it would be Oliver Wendell Holmes Jr. While some of Holmes's contemporaries saw in common law precedent a reflection of a natural universal reason, as Harvard Law School Dean Christopher Columbus Langdell put it, the "logical coherence of legal rules" showing through any correct array of precedents, Holmes saw law as a product of the historical conditions in which the courts, the lawyers, and the litigants lived. His famous aphorism that "the life of the law has not been logic, it has been experience," framed in answer to Langdell, would become the credo of the realist school of jurisprudence in the early twentieth century and remains the most-quoted phrase in modern Anglo-American jurisprudence. Holmes believed that "[t]he felt necessities of the time, the prevalent political and moral theories, institutions of public policy, avowed or unconscious, even the prejudices that judges share with their fellow-men" are the pillars of the law. Holmes, wounded three times serving in the Union Army during the Civil War, knew whereof he spoke. For then, competing versions of human liberty and constitutional law played out on the battlefield. Holmes had seen and felt how history and law collaborated to send some men to an early grave and gave others their freedom from bondage.[3]

This collaboration of law and history was the centerpiece of the "law and society" approach to the study of law after World War II. Pioneered by law professors and historians at the University of Wisconsin, the movement insisted that legal history be regarded as a product of the larger social, political, economic, and cultural life. Law was not autonomous, and change within it was not *sui generis*. Law was a dependent variable, shaped by change outside of the legal academy, the courts, and the texts. "The central point remains, law is a product of social forces, working in society." If law does not work for that society, it does not have "survival value." The external view of law and society features "a commitment to empirical observation and scientific measurement . . . to objectivity and neutrality." Law and society bids its followers to compile detailed observations about trends and shifts in the practice and impact of law—a study of law from the bottom up that includes legislators and legislation in its purview. As G. Edward White has written of his own journey from first to third edition of *The American Judicial Tradition*, "In the interval . . . the interest of scholars, students, and judges in the historical dimensions of law have grown dramatically, with the result that I have many more colleagues . . . working on projects in legal and constitutional history." Their explorations of both doctrine and social context had broadened his own and reached out into the wider world of historical scholarship.[4]

"Law Office History"

Although law and history in Anglo-American systems of jurisprudence are ready collaborators in the enterprise of legal history, the results of that collaboration have been subject to criticism from both sides of the academic aisle. Often dismissed by other scholars under the somewhat snide rubric of "law office history," criticisms of the conversation between law and history take a variety of forms. For example, law teachers in the "critical legal studies" movement, active from the 1970s to the 1990s, claimed that the tie between precedent and history was uncertain at best and deceitful at worst. Judges could select any of a multitude of lines of precedent and claim that history dictated their decisions. The "crits'" targets included liberals or "mainstream" thinkers whose views were "corrosive," "often wholly unreflecting, unselfconscious," because they did not question the very nature of "contingency" in the evolution of law. In other words, mainstream liberal legal history was either too uncritical of the phenomena it describes or an apologist for the existing legal system.[5]

The "crits," as they called themselves, were joined by mainstream legal historians in the attack on those judges and their allies in the law schools who claimed that the original intent of the framers of the Constitution and other laws should dictate the outcome of cases. "Courts should accordingly determine how the provisions were understood at the time they were ratified, and that understanding should guide decisions." The judge's reading of that intent dictates his opinion in constitutional litigation. Originalism originated with a speech by then–U.S. Attorney General Edwin Meese to the American Bar Association in 1985. He called for a jurisprudence of original intent, an inherently conservative proposal because the originators of the Constitution's language accepted slavery, opposed women's rights, and viewed Indians as a demonic menace. The problem with this version of law and history was that no one could be sure what James Madison or any other of the framers was thinking at the time. A later version of originalism proposed by U.S. Supreme Court Justice Antonin Scalia, sometimes called plain meaning originalism, dropped the requirement that jurists peer inside James Madison's head and bid them look instead at contemporary dictionary meanings of the Constitution's words. The problem with this program was that the first American dictionary did not appear until 1828, when all but a few of the framers had gone to their reward. Obviously, this version of law and history was as unappetizing to the historians as it should have been to judges. Despite some jurists' avowed fidelity to an interpretative strategy of "original meaning" or "original intent," historians know that the meanings that framers see in words and their intent in choosing words do not determine how those words will be read by later generations. Originalism assumes not only an objectivity that would make most working historians uncomfortable; it assumes a level of confidence in the historical findings that historians themselves would not share. In short, as a mode of constitutional interpretation, originalism is not very historical. "New values are invented and old ones given new content."[6]

A still more potent criticism of the collaboration of law and history regards legal history in the law school and on the bench as indifferent to time and place, a carryover from classical jurisprudence. According to what may be called the internalist or doctrinal approach long favored by most law professors, law evolved within itself as judges, jurists, and lawyers struggled to make the law fit a changing world. Accounts of law from the inside required specialized language and technical expertise. Alan Watson, a comparative law expert and law professor, explained: "[M]y often repeated argument [is] that legal development—in the broadest sense of law: the structure of the system, its major divisions, the approach to the sources of law, and the legal rules themselves—owes a great deal to the legal tradition and, to a marked degree, is independent of social, political, and economic factors." Bernard Schwartz, like Watson a law professor, put it this way in his history of American law: "[T]he story of American law is the story of the great lawyers and judges in our past." Some leading advocates of the internalist school conceptualized the story of law as a succession of periods or stages. Each stage or period will see the rise of a dominant style of judging and lawmaking. In 1960, law professor Karl Llewellyn proposed three major periods of legal thinking that he thought characterized the evolution of American law. Llewellyn's periods were "a way of thought and work . . . an on-going of doctrine . . . slowish [in] movement but striking in style."[7]

When historical evidence is "mined" to support one side in a lawsuit, or taken out of context to fit arbitrary legal categories, or cited without appropriate cautions in a lawyer's brief or a judge's opinion or a congressional debate on prospective legislation, both history and law are ill treated. "Many lawyers cannot see any difference at all between law and history, assuming that history is engaged in 'court like' activities of fact-finding and telling, and that historians and lawyers' practices are identical." Because of the limitations of space in legal briefs and judicial opinions, and the demands that the lawyer or judge come down on one side or another of the issue, law office history of this type often omits nuance and qualification, context and counter-examples.[8]

Historians concerned about the use of history in judicial opinions have on occasion tangled with judges. The most notorious controversy concerned Supreme Court Justice Hugo Black, a voracious reader of history, and the Pulitzer Prize–winning historian Leonard Levy. Black thought that the First Amendment barred Congress from punishing political opinions and said so in his opinions for the Court. Levy's *Legacy of Suppression: Freedom of Speech and Press in Early America* (1960) argued that many of the congressmen who voted for the First Amendment assumed it barred only prior censorship. At the time, Black told friends that he feared Levy's work would destroy the First Amendment. Levy later wrote that Black "was innocent of history when he did not distort it or invent it." Nonetheless, when Levy revised his book, he changed the title to *The Emergence of a Free Press*.[9]

Such controversies bespeak an uneasy alliance of law and history. Legal history so formulated might fill a gap in a law school curriculum or lend spurious authority to a citation in a judicial opinion but does not impress most academic historians. The result was that legal history remained for many years a kind of backwater in history departments, its shoreline littered with clever law review articles that no practicing historian regarded highly, much less cited, and casebook squibs that had neither beginning nor end but presented bits and pieces of appellate cases floating in timeless ether.

Consultants and Expert Witnesses

The collaboration of history and law in the courtroom appears indifferent to such academic caviling, for in the past few years, more and more historians have found employment as consultants and expert witnesses in civil law cases. These historians do contract work for law firms to prepare materials supporting their side in a lawsuit. The rewards are considerable—the hourly rate is mid–three figures and the hours can pile up. At first, historians provided these services without pay. The southern historians John Hope Franklin and C. Vann Woodward and the constitutional historian Alfred Kelly helped the NAACP deal with historical questions in *Brown v. Board of Education* (1954). In the 1960s and 1970s, historians worked for lawyers representing Indian tribes in their efforts to regain ancestral lands and for states quarreling with one another over boundary lines and water rights. More recently, they have provided research and testified in voting rights (reapportionment) cases, and suits involving the dangers of tobacco products, lead paint, and asbestos. There is a corporation that recruits and trains historians for this occupation and supplies their names to law firms. More informal networks within the historical profession helped to recruit the more than fifty historians who assist defendants in tobacco litigation.[10]

Like the expert witnesses in the civil rights cases, some historians called into service as expert witnesses truly believed in their cause. J. Morgan Kousser, who spent more than two decades testifying for racial minorities in voting rights cases, regarded the experience as "affording opportunities to tell the truth and do good at the same time." Other historians were not so pleased with their experience. Alfred Kelly, whose expert witnessing helped the Legal Defense Fund of the NAACP win *Brown v. Board of Education*, later recalled, "[H]ere I was, caught between my own ideals as a historian and what these people [the LDF] in New York wanted and needed." Jonathan D. Martin, who holds a Ph.D. in history, is a lawyer, and most recently served as law clerk to a federal district court judge, agreed: "The adversary process requires lawyers to spin the law and facts to serve their clients; lawyers are not expected, or even permitted, to be balanced and impartial. Historians, by contrast, should be open to all evidence they might encounter, and they accentuate the very ambiguities, contradictions, and inconsistencies that lawyers work doggedly within ethical bounds to hide or to smooth over." The historian David Rothman explained his own dilemma: "To enter the courtroom is to do many things, but it is not to do history. The essential attributes that we treasure most about historical inquiry must be left outside the courtroom door." But Rothman thought that historians should enter the fray when they thought they could make a genuine contribution to the briefs, or because they had a vital interest in the outcome of the case.[11]

The historian hired by a law firm as a research consultant or an expert witness must accept certain constraints. As Douglas R. Littlefield, the head of an agency putting historians and law firms together, explained to one gathering of historians, historians acting as consultants or expert witnesses for a law firm on a particular case seek answers to only the precise questions that the lawyers ask. The historian is thus narrowly bound to the role of detective. All findings must lead back to the questions rather than out into a wider context of events and people. As a rule, historians are trained to follow their research, wherever it leads, developing and answering new questions as they arise. Thus historical scholarship advances. Historians acting in the role of consultants or expert witnesses may chafe at the constraint of serving a law firm's client, but because the opposing counsel and their experts will be reading the deposition, affidavit, or other form of report of the consultant, he or she must be certain that the findings leave no loose ends that the other side can exploit. In effect, this often limits the historian to source mining—looking for those facts that support the version of the case for which the consultant has been hired. The consultant may not fabricate facts or lie, in part because of this adversarial nature of litigation. Nothing is worse for the consultant or the law firm than its historical evidence's being proved false. Incompleteness is another matter. Historians are trained to contextualize. Historians acting as consultants or expert witnesses are coached how to decontextualize.[12]

More constraining is the second requirement that Littlefield noted: no reference to secondary sources. Only primary sources are to be cited in the historian's account for the law firm. Secondary sources—other historians' views of the same body of evidence—undermine the authority of the consultant. His or her reading of the evidence becomes one perspective among many instead of the only conclusion that a reasonable person could reach. By contrast, historians are trained to read their colleagues' and predecessors' accounts, fitting new findings into established categories. The exception to this rule is that the consultant must be aware of the other party's presentation of the evidence and be prepared to counter it. Thus the only two secondary sources in play are those of the opposing counsels' experts.

A final injunction Littlefield offered was a ban on publication. In criminal cases, the arguments of counsel, including the presentation of incriminating and exculpating evidence, are matters of public record. In civil cases, the findings of the historical consultants belong to the law firms (so-called work product) and may be seen by the other party and by the court, or by a jury if one is impaneled to hear the case at trial, but are not matters of public record. Ordinarily, historians strive to publish their findings, for that is the purpose of scholarship, while consultants work "for hire" and have no control over their reports, save to respond to questioning by their own and opposing counsel.

To this expert's account of the constraints on the collaboration of history and law, I can add an anecdote of my own. I have participated in the drafting of a number of *amicus curiae* ("friends of the court") briefs in gun control cases. My contributions to the argument consisted of adding bits of historical evidence. Sometimes the lawyer in charge of the brief found these useful and included them, but on other occasions, relevant evidence was excluded because it might be interpreted by the other side to aid its cause. In conversations with other historians, I find they experienced similar frustration with the limitations that legal advocacy imposes on historical exposition. But the rules of the game are not set by the historians.

However, in one area of law practice calling upon historians as consultants and expert witnesses, historians have gone beyond the role of hireling. Reparations for the victims of historical injustices call on historians for their expertise and lawyers for the practical experience, a collaboration that has yielded remarkable results outside of the courtroom.

Reparations

The concept of reparations is a legal one, derived from a branch of jurisprudence called equity. Long ago, the equity courts were rivals to the common law courts in England, the former held by the king's secretary, or chancellor, and the latter presided over by the king's judges. Deriving their basic precepts from older ideas of doing justice in individual cases where going to law offered no relief, the equity courts helped both the rich and the poor gain the ear of the king. Procedure in the courts of equity was far simpler and more accessible than procedure in the law courts. In law, the writ that started the case was a Latin formula, and no case could be brought that did not fit one of the preexisting categories of writs. In equity, the petitioner made a complaint in ordinary language and named a remedy. Unlike the law courts, where evidence was presented at trial, in equity the parties took depositions and presented them in court. This was the forerunner of modern "discovery" rules. The equity courts had jurisdiction over the persons in the dispute while the law courts had jurisdiction over disputed property. The chancellors might order a wide array of remedies, including injunctions. These were commands to the parties to do or not do some act. The injunctive relief of the court of equity is the grandparent of the civil rights injunction, as today all federal courts are courts of both equity and law.[13]

Restitution, a form of equitable relief, was designed to give back to aggrieved parties what had unjustly been taken from them. Thus if a contract worker had largely but not wholly completed a task and was denied any payment because he or she failed to fulfill the terms of the contract, an equitable suit for restitution would gain the worker payment for the services he or she had performed. The essence of restitution is "to prevent the defendant from being unjustly enriched." What if the defendant stripped the innocent of his or her possessions down to the gold in his or her teeth, or grew rich on the forced labor of others? Would the petitioner in equity-seeking restitution not be entitled to it? History offers many cases of this very injustice, and the collaboration of law and history affords the descendants and survivors of those so deprived a remedy. This kind of remedy would and could not be the making whole of the victims in every case of historical injustice, for in most of the cases the victims have gone to their final reward. History retells the story of their plight, however, and historians and lawyers can collaborate in gaining the victims some measure of justice by telling their stories.[14]

Reparations can reach back into the distant past. The trigger for reparations for this kind of harm is proof of past injustice with continuing consequences in the present. Reparations may be financial. In 1971, congressional acts provided $1 billion in reparations, along with 44 million acres of land, to Alaskan native peoples. Courts returned tribal lands to other native peoples throughout the 1970s and 1980s. After a lawsuit seeking an equitable remedy, Japanese Americans interned during World War II were given reparations by Congress in 1988 to the tune of $1.6 billion (or $20,000 for every survivor of the camps). Historical records and historical research were crucial in determining the amount and the recipients of these reparations, and historians played a pivotal role.[15]

An even more extensive reparations relief program responded to the Holocaust and its victimization of the Jews. In 1952, the Israeli government began a long debate over the proposed Holocaust reparations offer that West Germany had broached. Some then, as now, thought that reparations were either inadequate or unnecessary. In September 1952, however, Israel and West Germany signed a reparations pact that "would provide $715 million in goods and services to the State of Israel as compensation for taking in survivors; $110 million to the Claims Conference for programs to finance the relief, rehabilitation, and resettlement of Jewish Holocaust survivors; and direct reparations to selected individuals over a 12-year period. Germany was once compensating 275,000 survivors."[16]

The terms of the reparations were negotiable. According to the Associated Press, in 2007 "Israeli Holocaust survivors asked Germany's finance minister Thursday [November 21] to improve a reparations arrangement set up a half-century ago, but he said no additional money would be paid. Survivors reasoned the original 1952 accord with Israel did not account for their unexpected longevity or apply to tens of thousands of Holocaust victims who came to Israel following the Soviet Union's collapse." Crucial was the concept of payment to survivors for what they had lost, a restitution remedy familiar in equity suits. "Germany has paid an estimated $25 billion in reparations to Israeli Holocaust survivors" over the years, and "more than $700 million in goods and services to the Israeli government."[17]

What keeps the Holocaust reparations question alive is not just the political clamor of the survivors or the legal expertise of their counsel but the historical memory of the Holocaust. Historical teaching can restore what reparations cannot repay. At Yad Vashem, the Holocaust museum in Jerusalem, and at Holocaust museums in Washington, Dallas, Los Angeles, St. Petersburg/Tampa Bay, Richmond, and Chicago, physical, visual, and text displays remind visitors of the horrors of the camps. The Holocaust is taught in more than 1,000 colleges in the United States and around the world, and in high school curricula nationally. The words of the victims are indelibly printed on the minds and in the hearts of students. Without the historical memory of the Holocaust, the reparations would be just a redistribution of wealth. With the historical memory, they are an example of the power of history and law, working in partnership, to repair injustice. Thus the lesson of the Holocaust is that past injustice is a present obligation, a lesson that the collaboration of law and history promoted.

The restitution that lessons of the Holocaust memorialized, taught in schools, and shared widely with various publics would not be possible without the scholarship of the historians. In turn, historical scholarship would be worth little as restitution without its dissemination beyond the halls of academe into the legal realm. It is in the confluence of the professional historian's findings and a willingness to trust history in the courts and congresses that the part restitution plays in the Holocaust story gains its deepest meaning.

Reparations for American slavery and the slave trade are an even larger challenge to the collaboration of law and history, for slavery in America was impossible without the active assistance of the law. In other words, not only was the law complicit in the creation of slavery, it was only with the active assistance of legislatures and courts that slaveholders could keep millions of men and women in bondage. Slavery was the most divisive political question at the federal constitutional convention of 1787. There the founders, with the exceptions of anti-slavery spokesmen Elbridge Gerry, Rufus King, and Gouverneur Morris, sought a compromise between freedom and free labor, on the one hand, and slavery and slave labor on the other. The federal Constitution never mentioned slavery, but provided for a three-fifths portion of total slaves to count in states' apportionment, allowed the despised international slave trade to continue until 1808, and, most controversially, provided for the rendition of those "owing labor" in one state who fled to be forcibly returned to the state from which they had escaped. Slavery was to be legal where state law established it and illegal when state law barred it.[18]

In slavery cases like *Prigg v. Pennsylvania* (1842), the federal courts not only acceded to the peculiar institution, they protected it. Justice Joseph Story, who wrote the decision of the High Court in *Prigg*, was a professional from head to toe, a law professor at Harvard as well as a respected member of the High Court, and the author of treatises on the Constitution and other legal subjects. He abhorred the institution of slavery and said so in his private correspondence. He nevertheless recognized slavery's constitutional posture—the Rendition Clause dictated "No person held to service or labour in one state under the laws thereof, escaping into another, shall in consequence of any law or regulation therein, be discharged from such service or labour; but shall be delivered up, on claim of the party to whom such service or labour may be due." Story felt obliged by his professional duty as a judge to opine that the state of Pennsylvania could not try a slave catcher for kidnaping an alleged runaway. "Few questions which have ever come before this Court involve more delicate and important considerations; and few upon which the public at large may be presumed to feel a more profound and pervading interest. We have accordingly given them our most deliberate examination; and it has become my duty to state the result to which we have arrived, and the reasoning by which it is supported." As he wrote to a friend shortly after the decision was announced and Massachusetts anti-slavery voices rose to condemn him: "You know full well that I have ever been opposed to slavery. But I take my standard of duty as a judge from the Constitution."[19]

Slavery was ended by the Thirteenth Amendment to the federal Constitution, but its lasting impact, flowing through the Jim Crow system of state-sponsored legal segregation that replaced slavery in much of the post–Civil War nation, can still be felt in the twenty-first century. Again it was a case of unjust enrichment. By 2008, many major corporations whose founders benefited from the slave trade or from funds gained in the slave trade offered formal apologies. One of these was Brown University, whose eponymous founder, the Brown family, was a major player in the American slave trade.

Reparations to the victims of the slave trade would involve an astronomical amount of money, but a restitution remedy was available. Payouts were not an option, but historical reparations could include an attempt to retrieve the history and apply it to the remedy. As such, the Brown version of restitution was a full-fledged partnership of legal concept and historical pedagogy by restoring the historical understanding of the contributions of slaves to history of the nation.

Brown University's coverage of the reparations debate at Brown was exhaustive and, though in some ways self-serving, gave evidence of the seriousness with which the university took its legal and historical obligations. In 2003, Brown University President Ruth J. Simmons appointed a Steering Committee on Slavery and Justice to investigate the University's historical relationship to slavery and the transatlantic slave trade. On October 18, 2006, the committee reported its findings. These were released to the public. Using history itself as a kind of restitution brought together the skills of the historian, preparing and displaying the materials, and the conceptual virtuosity of the law. For "the committee was also asked to reflect on the meaning of this history in the present, on the complex historical, political, legal, and moral questions posed by any present-day confrontation with past injustice."[20]

The last three pages of the eighty-eight-page report specified the recommendations of the Committee on Slavery and Justice. Every one of the recommendations rested upon the assumption that public awareness and expert judgment were both essential components of legal idea of restitution:

Acknowledgment . . . to acknowledge formally and publicly the participation of many of Brown's founders and benefactors in the institution of slavery and the transatlantic slave trade, as well as the benefits that the University derived from them.

Tell the truth in all its complexity. . . . The appointment of the steering committee and the various public programs it sponsored have already done a great deal to create awareness of a history that had been largely erased from the collective memory of our University and state. . . . [S]ponsor public forums, on campus and off, to allow anyone with an interest in the steering committee's work to respond to, reflect upon, and criticize the report.

Memorialization . . . The challenge, easier to articulate than to accomplish, is to create a living site of memory, inviting reflection and fresh discovery without provoking paralysis or shame. We believe that Brown can and should answer this challenge. We recommend that the University undertake to create a slave trade memorial to recognize its relationship to the transatlantic trade and the importance of this traffic in the history of Rhode Island.

Public programming aimed at both the University and the wider community; a significant educational outreach component, including workshops and curriculum development, to help teachers integrate topics related to slavery and justice into their classrooms.[21]

There were other commission proposals, part of a comprehensive attempt to keep the memory of the horrors of slavery and the slave trade alive in the minds of the coming generations. Again, the essence of the collaboration of law and history was more history, better history, taught more broadly. While this list of reparations did not arrange to repay unpaid wages or restore lost goods, it did seek to do equity in a broader way. If equity reunites what past injustice has torn asunder, the institutional support of historical studies of slavery and the slave trade restores something of great value to the descendants of slavery's victims. It gives them back a history. It reminds everyone, white and black, of the contributions of the slaves to the American economy, of the ways in which slaves created their own culture and family life in the midst of their travails, and of the courage of those who risked all to flee slavery or to rebel against it. The legacy of the past can be reformed by knowing more about the past. By revisiting the injustice and reminding people today of the continuing impact of the past on the present, restitution enables history and law to alter that impact. Restitution reunites what had been unjustly severed, the story of one part of the people from the rest. It makes history whole again.

* * *

Law is the most potent of all of history's modern-day collaborators because good law's roots lie in thoughtful historical assay. True, that relationship has a "complex and contingent" application in law cases, as different players in the legal arena read precedent, precept, obligation, and legal standards in varying ways. But this much cannot be disputed: All of Clio's other companions can depart from history (to be sure, at their peril), but a law uprooted from history would be arbitrary at best and tyranny at worst. By contrast, working in harmony, law and history can recover hitherto lost individual rights and recognize the past contributions of even the most marginal of groups.[22]

Conclusion

An Answer?

In these pages I have argued that without their tie to religion, the first histories would have had little purpose. Without the infusion of philosophical rigor, history would have taught little of lasting value. Without the introduction of social sciences, history might have been dismissed as mere antiquarianism, like its subject matter a relic of a bygone world. Without literary art, history would not be worth reading. Without biographies, history would have had far fewer readers. Without policy studies, history would have little significance for the very people who have the greatest impact on our world. Without its ties to law, history could never provide remedy for the tragedies that its students uncover. History today would not exist without these collaborators, but history is more than the product of all these interactions—the value added to culture by the study of history itself.

First, unlike all of its modern companions, history belongs to everyone. Everyone has a history. Everyone knows some history. As Harvard's Laurel Thatcher Ulrich told an interviewer not long ago, "We need to have a little a bit of humility to recognize [that] people can do what they want to with the past. Historians do not own history." Or, as former AHA President Eric Foner explained, "Who owns history? Everyone and no one."[1]

Second, unlike some of the more dogmatic of Clio's companions, history is self-examining. Historians do not flinch from this often painful inward look. For the members of the American Historical Association's Professional Division, 2004 was a particularly unpleasant time for the profession. Scandal was abroad. To try to respond, the division refined the *Statement on Standards of Professional Conduct* first written in 1985. The revision spoke to growing dismay in the media and the profession about the trustworthiness of history and historians. In part it reads: "Historians strive constantly to improve our collective understanding of the past through a complex process of critical dialogue—with each other, with the wider public, and with the historical record.... Historians cannot successfully do this work without mutual trust and respect. By practicing their craft with integrity, historians acquire a reputation for trustworthiness that is arguably their single most precious professional asset." Trust comes from self-examination, from candid and constructive criticism within the profession, and from the awareness that historians have a larger audience than their peers.[2]

If historians are fallible, there is no dogma in history itself, no vested interest, no hidden agenda, no sacred forms—not any that really matter—that are proof against revision. For time will always change our angle of repose, and time's handmaiden, hindsight, will sharpen our judgments. As J. H. Plumb wrote in *The Death of the Past*, "[T]he generalizations of western history were the refined end-product of years of patient argument in which generalizations and fresh facts had created an ever more sophisticated dialogue."[3]

Third, worthwhile historical scholarship is based on a gentle gradualism, a piling up of factual knowledge, a sifting and reframing of analytical models, an ongoing collective enterprise that unites generation after generation of scholars to their readers and listeners. For "Our thinking of the world, our imagination (and we imagine and see together) anthropomorphizes and humanizes everything, even inanimate things, just as our exploration of the universe is inevitably geocentric" and "our consciousness, our central situation in space, cannot be separated from our consciousness of time." We think in historical terms because "we are the stuff of history."[4]

In the end, it is that last, unique quality is what makes our historical labors so vital to us, the subjects of history. History is about people and its judgments are about people. It is because history, in the last analysis, is what we share with everyone else. This is what elevates history above its collaborators, making history more than just the sum of those parts. For more than any particular religious outlook, philosophical theory, social science finding, literary trope, biographical insight, policy stance, or legal program, history is the judgment of people by people. It mirrors our own preoccupations and values. It grows wiser, and sometimes sadder, with us. It reflects our hopes and passes judgment on our deeds.

By this I do not mean the vulgar relativism that reduces all historical knowing to passing fads and contemporary biases, that puckishly dismisses the deeper value of history by "historicizing" the discipline itself, "to see all historical accounts as imprisoned in time and space" and all historical judgment as the expression of local and self-serving ideologies. The judgment of history is the judgment that we pass upon ourselves. It is against our own standards that we measure our predecessors'. Insofar as historical knowledge reflects the preoccupations and values of our own time and place, what we say of others is a mirror of what we see in ourselves. Often that judgment is a severe one, unrelenting and unchangeable, though all might wish it not so. But that judgment may also liberate us from the cavils of our own time, revealing to us our place in the long span of human development.[5]

The art of history, the science of history, the philosophy of history, and a religious view of history all coincide in this single place: Historical studies would be impossible without a "just and humane" view of people in the past. "That slavery is wrong, that man has rights, are coming to be recognized—not as generalizations—but as presuppositions of history; so that the nearer societies approach these norms the higher their status in value." What follows from this judgment? As Carl Becker wrote in 1915, "By liberalizing the mind, by deepening the sympathies, by fortifying the will, history enables us to control, not society, but ourselves." That is not all, however. For a history that remained a private treasure would be a poor thing indeed. The judgment of history is more than something we keep to ourselves. John Hope Franklin put it best: "'One might argue that the historian is the conscience of the nation, if honesty and consistency are factors that nurture the conscience."[6]

At the end of the movie *Kingdom of Heaven*, Balian, the defender of Jerusalem against the besieging Saracens, asks the Saracen commander Salahadin, "What is Jerusalem worth?" Salahadin, offered the city in return for safe conduct for its inhabitants, shrugs his shoulders and answers, "Nothing." As he walks away, he turns, smiles, raises both fists in triumph, and says, "Everything!" The movie's history is not very accurate (except for the reproduction of period costumes and weapons), but the scene is deeply moving. For Salahadin has told us a great deal about history. If he did not care about Jerusalem's past, possessing it would be worthless. It is only because of its past, and the meaning of that past to him, that it is worth everything.

I hope I have made a plausible case that history stands, and should stand, at the center of our quest for a truly humane spirit, that Clio is surrounded and honored by her companions' attention. Religion can console the wounded heart; philosophy sate the restless mind; social science requite the inquiring brain; literature and biography pleasure the spirit; policy studies teach us lessons; and law reform our ways; but only history can do all of these—if we but trust it. History matters because we want it to matter; because it honors human longing and endeavor, and doing it rightly becomes a grave command we issue to ourselves.

NOTES

Notes to the Introduction

1. Leopold von Ranke, *Histories of the Latin and Germanic Nations* (1824) quoted in Richard J. Evans, *In Defense of History* (New York: Norton, 2000), 14.
2. "The Study of History in Schools: A Report to the American Historical Association by the Committee of Seven" [1898], reproduced at www.historians.org/pubs/archives/CommitteeofSeven/ReportValue.cfm. I use the term "the West" to denote western Europe and the United States. Peter N. Stearns, "Why Study History" (1998) http://www.historians.org/pubs/free/WhyStudyHistory.htm.
3. Philip D. Curtin, *The World and the West: The European Challenge and the Overseas Response in the Age of Empire* (Cambridge: Cambridge University Press, 2000), x; J. H. Plumb, *The Death of the Past* [1969] (2nd ed. London: Palgrave, 2004), 19; Evans, *In Defense Of History*, 25.
4. Martin Duberman, *The Uncompleted Past* (New York: Dutton, 1971), 356; John Tosh, *The Pursuit of History* 5th ed. (Harlow: Longman, 2010), 7; Daniel J. Boorstin, *Cleopatra's Nose: Essays on the Unexpected* (New York: Random House, 1994), x; Margaret MacMillan, *Dangerous Games: The Uses and Abuses of History* (New York: Modern Library, 2010), 170; Anthony Grafton, "History Under Attack" *Perspectives on History* 49 (January 2011), 5; James Loewen, *Lies My Teacher Told Me* rev. ed. (New York: Touchstone, 2007), 9; Keith Jenkins, *Re-Thinking History* (London: Routledge, 2003), 34, 67.
5. Henry Ford quoted in David Kyvig and Myron A. Marty, *Nearby History: Exploring the Past Around You* (2nd ed. Lanham, Md.: Rowman and Littlefield, 2000), 1; George Bernard Shaw, *The Devil's Disciple* [1903] in John A. Bertolini, ed., *Man and Superman and Three Other Plays* (New York: Barnes and Noble, 2004), 283; "one damn thing after another" in G. R. Elton, *The Practice of History* (London: Methuen, 1967), 40; Francis Fukuyama, *The Death of History and the Last Man* (New York: Free Press, 1992), 136. And now for something entirely different—the academic historian as staff writer for literary magazines. The parade is led by Sean

Wilentz, a chaired professor at Princeton, who is a contributing editor at *The New Republic*; followed by Jon Weiner, who teaches at University of California, Irvine, and does a column for *The Nation*; and not least by Jill Lepore, who interrupts her duties teaching at Harvard to publish regularly in *The New Yorker*. But befitting the climate of opinion these days, their writings are often handwringing, dour, and censorious. It appears that everyone (but us) is misusing history.

6. Lynne V. Cheney, *Telling the Truth: Why Our Culture and Our Country Have Stopped Making Sense—And What We Can Do About It* (New York: Touchstone, 1995), 114; Cheney, "The End of History," *Wall Street Journal* October 20, 1994, A26.

7. Newt Gingrich, reprinted in *Congressional Record* 104 Cong. 1st sess. February 8, 1995, E301.

8. Gary B. Nash, Charlotte Crabtree, and Ross E. Dunn, *History on Trial: Culture Wars and the Teaching of the Past* rev. ed. (New York: Vintage, 2000), 158; Nash, "Reflections on the National History Standards," *Forum*, 1997, www-personal. umich.edu/~mlassite/discussions261/nash.html.

9. Jefferson to Madison, February 27, 1826, *The Writings of Thomas Jefferson*, ed. Paul L. Ford (New York, 1892–99), 10:327; President George W. Bush at his final press conference, January 12, 2009, quoted by Leonard Doyle, "History Will Be My Judge" *Independent* (London), January 13, 2009, p. 22. Vernon Burton, author of *The Age of Lincoln*, told me that President Bush wrote him to thank him for a copy and made the comparison. Burton to the author, August 28, 2010; Frank Kermode, *The Sense of an Ending: Studies in the Theory of Fiction* rev. ed. (New York: Oxford University Press, 2000), 97; Hayden White, "The Burden of History" in White, *Tropics of Discourse* (Baltimore: Johns Hopkins University Press, 1966), 41; Tosh, *The Pursuit of History*, 13.

10. I attempted a somewhat more conventional approach in *The Historians' Paradox: A Philosophy of History for Our Time* (New York: New York University Press, 2008) and concluded that history was possible in the same way the building of a bridge was possible when the far side of the bridge is shrouded in mist. Stephen Leacock, like Benchley, is rarely read today. He was a Canadian academic political scientist and armchair philosopher, and a popular humorist. He and Benchley much admired each other's essays. Leacock died in 1944, a year before Benchley. Lord Ronald is a character in *Nonsense Novels* [1911] (New York: Dodd, Mead, 1922) and leaps onto his horse on page 73.

11. MacMillan, *Dangerous Games*, x. A comparative disciplinary approach to historical knowing similar to (though far more complex than) the one assayed herein: Dominick Lacapra, *Writing History, Writing Trauma* (Baltimore: Johns Hopkins University Press, 2000), 3, n.4.

12. David Harlan, *The Degradation of American History* (Chicago: University of Chicago Press, 1997), xxxii.

NOTES TO CHAPTER 1 >> 157

Notes to Chapter 1
  1. Michael Winship, a historian's historian of Tudor–Stuart English and New England puritanism.
  2. Baruch Halpern, *The First Historians: The Hebrew Bible and History* (New York: Harper & Row, 1988), 20; Ernst Breisach, *Historiography: Ancient, Medieval, and Modern* (3rd ed. Chicago: University of Chicago Press, 2007), 126–27.
  3. Michael J. White, "Stoic Natural Philosophy" in *Cambridge Companion to the Stoics*, ed. Brad Imwood (Cambridge: Cambridge University Press, 2003), 137; Axel Michaels, *Hinduism: Past and Present* (Princeton, N.J.: Princeton University Press, 2004), 28, 29, 305.
  4. Modern exponents of the importance of myth as a spiritual foundation of everyday life include such diverse figures as Joseph Campbell, Mircea Eliade, and Carl Jung. See, e.g., "New Myth" *Oxford Companion to World Mythology*, ed. David Adams Leeming (Oxford: Oxford University Press, 2005), 283–85.
  5. Gregory of Tours, *The History of the Franks*, ed. and trans. Lewis Thorpe (New York: Penguin, 1974), 67. This "large and vital text" was one of the first of the successor kingdoms to the Roman Empire. It is a true history by a historian, not merely a "storehouse of facts." Martin Heinzelman, "Introduction," *Gregory of Tours: History and Society in the Sixth Century* (Cambridge: Cambridge University Press, 2001), 1, 2.
  6. Bede, *The Ecclesiastical History of the English People*, trans. Bertram Colgrave, ed. Judith McClure and Roger Collins (Oxford: Oxford University Press, 1999), 16.
  7. Jean Froissart, *Chronicles*, trans. and ed. Geoffrey Brereton (New York: Penguin, 1978), 234, 233.
  8. A. F. S. Pearson, *Thomas Cartwright and Elizabethan Puritanism* (Cambridge: Cambridge University Press, 1925), 73; Edward Johnson, *Johnson's Wonder-Working Providence* [1654], ed. J. Franklin Jameson (New York: Scribner's, 1910), 40, 42, 43.
  9. John L. O'Sullivan, "The Great Nation of Futurity," *The United States Democratic Review* 6 No. 23 (1839), 430; Abraham Lincoln, Second Inaugural Address, March 4, 1865, in Ida M. Tarbell, *Selections from the Letters, Speeches, and State Papers of Abraham Lincoln* (New York: Ginn, 1911), 118.
 10. Steven J. Keillor, *God's Judgments: Interpreting History and the Christian Faith* (Downers Grove, Ill.: IVP Academic Press, 2007), 19.
 11. Moses Maimonides, *The Book of Knowledge: From the Mishneh Torah of Moses Maimonides*, trans. Helen M. Russell and J. Weinberg (Jersey City, N.J.: KTAV, 1985), 121.
 12. Charles Darwin, *On the Origin of Species* [1859] (6th corrected edition New York: Appleton, 1900), 2:267.
 13. David Quammen, *The Reluctant Mr. Darwin: An Intimate Portrait of Charles Darwin and the Making of His Theory of Evolution* (New York: Norton, 2009), 12.

14. American Museum of Natural History "Darwin" exhibition, November 2005, www.amnh.org/exhibitions/darwin/work/world.php; Quammen, *Reluctant Mr. Darwin*, 209–16; Adrian J. Desmond and James Moore, *Darwin* (New York: Norton, 1994), 522.

15. Charles Darwin, *The Descent of Man and Selection in Relation to Sex* (New York: American Dome, 1902), part 2, 781.

16. Richard Dawkins, *The Ancestor's Tale: A Pilgrimage to the Dawn of Evolution* (Boston: Houghton Mifflin, 2004), 1.

17. Richard Dawkins, *The God Delusion* (New York: Houghton Mifflin, 2006), 142, 190.

18. Charles Hodge, *What Is Darwinism?* (New York: Scribner's, 1874), 2:173; Poteat spoke in 1925, quoted in Mark Taylor Dalhouse, *An Island in the Lake of Fire: Bob Jones University, Fundamentalism, and the Separatist Movement* (Athens: University of Georgia Press, 1996), 33; Desmond and Moore, *Darwin*, 524–27.

19. "Dinosaurs" at www.creationism.org/topbar/dinosaurs.htm, the creationism.org web site; "Intelligent Design" at www.intelligentdesign.org/.

20. M. C. D'Arcy, *History: A Christian View* (New York: Farrar, Straus & Giroux, 1959), 16.

21. Voltaire, "The Clergyman and His Soul" in *The Works of Voltaire, A Contemporary Version*, ed. Tobias Smolett, trans. William Fleming (New York: DuMont, 1901), 2:18–19; Arnold J. Toynbee, *A Study of History: Volume 4, The Breakdown of Civilizations* [1939] (New York: Oxford University Press, 1962), 227; Peter Dickson, *Kissinger and the Meaning of History* (Cambridge: Cambridge University Press, 1978), 11, 12; Arthur M. Schlesinger Jr., Speech at Brown University, 1989, quoted in Garry Wills, *Under God: Religion and American Politics* (New York: Simon and Schuster, 2007), 87.

22. Stephen J. Gould, *Rocks of Ages: Science and Religion in the Fullness of Life* (New York: Ballantine, 1999), 4, 5, 84.

23. Ibid., 193, 195.

24. Russell Shorto, "How Christian Were the Founders?" *New York Times Magazine*, February 14, 2010.

25. Scott Horton, "Six Questions for Garry Wills on *What the Gospels Meant*," *Harpers Magazine*, March 15, 2008; Garry Wills, *What the Gospels Meant* (New York: Viking, 2008), 1.

26. Christopher Lasch, *The Minimal Self: Psychic Survival in Troubled Times* (New York: Norton, 1984), 18, 259; Eugene Genovese and Elizabeth Fox-Genovese, *The Mind of the Master Class: History and Faith in the Southern Slaveholders' Worldview* (New York: Cambridge University Press, 2005), 679.

27. Karen Armstrong, *The Case for God* (New York: Knopf, 2009), 318; Diarmaid MacCulloch, *Christianity: The First Three Thousand Years* (New York: Viking, 2010), 1016.

28. Morning service for Yom Kippur, "Let Us Proclaim the Sacred Power of This Day" Central Conference of American Rabbis, *Gates of Repentance* (New York, 1996), 312.

Notes to Chapter 2

1. Nicholas Phillipson, *David Hume: The Philosopher as Historian* (rev. ed. New Haven, Conn.: Yale University Press, 2012), 4; David Hume, *A Treatise of Human Nature* [1739] (Oxford: Clarendon Press, 1896), 55, 83.

2. Hume's history and his philosophy proceeded side by side, as he turned from one publishing project to another. To argue that he saw the two disciplines as fundamentally different because he saw causation as a human rather than a natural construct is to misconstrue his entire intellectual career.

3. Aviezer Tucker, "Introduction," in *Blackwell Companion to the Philosophy of History and Historiography* (Boston: Wiley-Blackwell, 2003), 3. Apparently, the cross-grained nature of the relationship is as old as history and philosophy themselves. See Ernst Breisach, *Historiography: Ancient, Medieval, and Modern* (3rd ed. Chicago: University of Chicago Press, 2007), 32.

4. Michael C. Lemon, *Philosophy of History: A Guide for Students* (London: Routledge, 2003), 36; Richard Braithwait, *A Survey of History* (London, 1638), 2; George Bancroft, *The History of the United States from the Discovery of the American Continent* [1834] (reprinted Boston: Little, Brown, 1844), 2: 345; Harlan, *Degradation*, xxxii, xxxiii.

5. Terry Pinkard, *Hegel: A Biography* (Cambridge: Cambridge University Press, 2001), 513–15.

6. Georg Hegel, *Hegel's Science of Logic*, trans. A. V. Miller (London: Routledge, 2002), 82.

7. The virtual conversation between the two men went on for decades as Marx firmed his own ideas. Frederick Copleson, *A History of Philosophy* (New York: Doubleday, 1962), 7: 308–10; Robert Nisbet, *History of the Idea of Progress* (2nd ed. New York: Transaction, 2004), 259–60; Francis Wheen, *Karl Marx: A Life* (New York: Norton, 2001), 21.

8. S. H. Rigby, *Marxism and History: A Critical Introduction* (Manchester: University of Manchester Press, 1998), 7; Karl Marx, *The Poverty of Philosophy* [1847], quoted in Howard Selsam and Harry Martel, eds., *Reader in Marxist Philosophy* (New York: International, 1963), 188.

9. Clayton R. Roberts, *The Logic of Historical Explanation* (University Park: Pennsylvania State University Press, 1996), 278.

10. Crane Brinton, *Nietzsche* (Cambridge, Mass.: Harvard University Press, 1941), 172.

11. Friedrich Nietzsche, *Beyond Good and Evil* [1886], trans. Walter Kaufmann (New York: Vintage, 1966), 42, 43.

12. Friedrich Nietzsche, *The Use and Abuse of History* (New York: Liberal Arts Press, 1873), 37–38, 33.

13. Nietzsche, *Beyond Good and Evil*, 202, 203, 204.

14. Walter Arnold Kaufmann, *Nietzsche: Philosopher, Psychologist, AntiChrist* (Princeton, N.J.: Princeton University Press, 2002), 150. Admirers of Nietzsche will not accept this conclusion and cite instead how modernist arts and writers found

inspiration in Nietzsche's call for cosmic creativity. Like the supplicants of the oracle at Delphi, readers of Nietzsche can take what they want from reading him.

15. Karl Popper, *The Poverty of Historicism* [1957] (2nd ed. London: Routledge, 2002), 46, 23; Popper, *The Open Society and Its Enemies* (New York: Harper, 1963), 2: 307.

16. Charles Beard, "Presidential Address: Written History as an Act of Faith," *American Historical Review* 39 (1933), 219; Jennifer Ratner-Rosenhagen, *American Nietzsche: A History of an Icon and His Ideas* (Chicago: University of Chicago Press, 2012), 27; Martin Gardner, "A Skeptical Look at Karl Popper," *Skeptical Inquirer*, 25 (2001), 13.

17. Joseph J. Ellis, *His Excellency: George Washington* (New York: Knopf, 2004), 3; Fred Anderson, *Crucible of War: The Seven Years' War and the Fate of Empire in British North America, 1754–1766* (New York: Knopf, 2000), 7; Peter Winch, *The Idea of a Social Science, and Its Relation to Philosophy* (London: Routledge, 1958), 3, 107, 123. Winch taught an introductory course in philosophy my sophomore year at the University of Rochester in which I enrolled, and though I did not realize it at the time, he has had a very profound influence on how I see history.

18. David Hackett Fischer, *Historians' Fallacies: Toward a Logic of Historical Thought* (New York: Harper, 1970), 79–80.

19. Gordon Wright, "History as a Moral Science," *American Historical Review* 81 (1976), 2, 4; Stanley Fish, *Save the World on Your Own Time* (New York: Oxford University Press, 2008), 14, 53, 142; Jane Kamensky, "Fighting Over Words," in Richard Wrightman Fox and Robert B. Westbrook, eds., *In the Face of the Facts: Moral Inquiry in American Scholarship* (New York: Cambridge University Press, 2002), 120.

20. Stephen Toulmin, *The Uses of Argument* [1958] (Cambridge: Cambridge University Press, 2003), 50, 52; William Thompson, *An Inquiry into the Principles of the Distribution of Wealth Most Conducive to Human Happiness* (London: W. S. Orr, 1850), xxvi–xxvii.

21. This and other quotations from this subsection, along with much of its text, taken by permission from Peter Charles Hoffer, *The Historians' Paradox: A Philosophy of History for Our Times* (New York: New York University Press, 2008), 11–12, 33.

22. Ibid., 29.

23. Roberts, *Historical Explanation*, 174.

24. Hoffer, *Historians' Paradox*, 12.

25. Fischer, *Historians' Fallacies*, 200, 78.

26. Christopher John Shields, *Aristotle* (London: Taylor and Francis, 2007), 66.

27. David Hume, *An Enquiry Concerning Human Understanding* [1748] (Chicago: Open Court, 1907), bk. 1, p. 221; Hume, *Treastise of Human Nature*, 146; Claudia M. Schmidt, *David Hume: Reason in History* (State College: Pennsylvania State University Press, 2004), 173. Hume did not make the modern distinction between epistemology (the study of knowledge) and linguistics (the study of language).

28. Immanuel Kant, *On History*, trans. Lewis White Beck (Indianapolis: Bobbs-Merrill, 1963), 143.

29. Karl Hempel, "Deductive and Probabilistic Explanation in Covering Laws," in *The Philosophy of Karl Hempel*, ed. James H. Fetzer (New York: Oxford University Press, 2001), 297 ff.

30. Roberts, *Historical Explanation*, 241.

31. Marie Swabey, *The Judgment of History* (New York: The Philosophical Library, 1954), 238, 240, 245.

32. Kamala Visweswaren, "The Interventions of Culture," in Robert Bernasconi, ed., *Race and Racism in Continental Thought* (Bloomington: Indiana University Press, 2003), 229; Franz Boas, *Anthropology and Modern Life* (New York: Norton, 1928), 19, 22.

33. Claude Lévi-Strauss, *Structural Anthropology*, trans. Claire Jacobson (New York: Basic, 1963), 65, 161; Lévi-Strauss, *Totemism*, trans. Rodney Needham (Boston: Beacon, 1971), 61.

34. Carl Jung, *Four Archetypes*, trans. Richard Francis Carrington Hull (3rd ed. London: Routledge, 2003), 13, 15.

35. Anna Green and Kathleen Troup, *The Houses of History: A Critical Reader in Twentieth-Century History and Theory* (New York: New York University Press, 1999), 89.

36. If so, then time to close this book now and toss it along with the rest of the history books on our shelves into the flames, along with treatises on metaphysics, theology tracts, and old "Pogo" comic strip anthologies. As the last of these options is unthinkable, perhaps the rest of the books should stay where they are.

37. But see Mark Day, *The Philosophy of History: An Introduction* (London: Continuum, 2008), 117–18 and after, questioning this project.

38. Wilhelm Dilthey, "Goethe and the Poetic Imagination" [1910], in *Works of Wilhelm Dilthey*, ed. and trans. Rudolf A. Makkreel and Frithjof Rodi (Princeton, N.J.: Princeton University Press, 1985), 4:251; Makkreel, *Dilthey: Philosopher of the Human Studies* (Princeton, N.J.: Princeton University Press, 1992), 26, 408.

39. Merle Curti, *The Growth of American Thought* (3rd ed. Edison, N.J.: Transaction, 1981), vii–viii.

40. Richard Hofstadter, *Anti-Intellectualism in American Life* (New York: Knopf, 1963), 4.

41. Ernst Breisach, *On the Future of History: The Postmodernist Challenge and Its Aftermath* (Chicago: University of Chicago Press, 2003), 6; D'Arcy, *History*, 15; Michael Stanford, *An Introduction to the Philosophy of History* (New York: Wiley, 1998), 4; Lemon, *Philosophy of History*, 8.

42. Donald Davidson, *Subjective, Intersubjective, Objective* (New York: Oxford University Press, 2001), 161.

Notes to Chapter 3

1. See, e.g., Stephen Toulmin, *The Uses of Argument* [1958] (Cambridge: Cambridge University Press, 2003), 50, 52 (historical statements are statements of probability, and historical scholarship is all about weighing probabilities).

2. Barbara Shapiro, *A Culture of Fact: England, 1550–1720* (Ithaca, N.Y.: Cornell University Press, 2000) 35, 37; John Lukacs, "Popular and Professional History," in Donald A. Yerxa, ed., *Recent Themes in Historical Thinking, Historians in Conversation* (Columbia: University of South Carolina Press, 2008), 44.

3. Bacon was generally accounted a man of genius in a century of genius, primarily for his contributions to philosophy of science. See Perez Zagorin, *Francis Bacon* (Princeton, N.J.: Princeton University Press, 1999), 222–23.

4. Francis Bacon, "The Advancement of Learning," in *Novum Organum* [1620] (Franklin Center, Pa.: Franklin Library, 1980), 89, 90, 91, 92, 95.

5. Francis Bacon, *Novum Organum* [1620], in *The Works of Francis Bacon*, ed. and trans. James Spedding, Robert Ellis, and Douglas Heath (Boston: Taggart, 1863), 8:77–78.

6. Peter Burke, *A Social History of Knowledge: From Gutenburg to Diderot* (New York: Wiley, 2000), 14, 15; Eve Rachele Sanders, *Gender and Literacy on Stage in Early Modern England* (Cambridge: Cambridge University Press, 1998), 143. Does literacy fundamentally change a person's abilities to function in modern society? Certainly, yes. But in premodern and early modern societies, the answer is not so clear.

7. S. W. Serjeantson, "Proof and Persuasion," *Cambridge History of Science, Volume 3: Early Modern Science* (Cambridge: Cambridge University Press, 2006), 175.

8. Charles C. Gillispie, *The Edge of Objectivity: An Essay in the History of Scientific Ideas* (Princeton, N.J.: Princeton University Press, 1960), 153; Charles de Secondat Montesquieu, *The Spirit of the Laws* [1752], trans. and ed. Anne M. Cohler (Cambridge: Cambridge University Press, 1989), 4; Auguste Comte, *The Positive Philosophy of Auguste Comte* [1853], trans. Harriet Martineau (London: G. Bell, 1896), 2:212.

9. Bury, Fustel, and von Ranke appeared in my dog-eared copy of Fritz Stern, ed., *The Varieties of History* (New York: Meridian, 1956), at 208, 178, and 55. The Johns Hopkins seminar room, "Historical Seminary Looking East" and "Historical Seminary Looking West" Johns Hopkins, 1887, was once to be found on the web at ndsu.edu/instruct/isem/489/adamshtml. On the craze for history as science, see John Burrow, *A History of Histories* (New York: Random House, 2009), 445–48, and Mark T. Gilderhus, *History and Historians: A Historiographical Introduction* (7th ed. Upper Saddle River, N.J.: Prentice Hall, 2010), 87.

10. R. G. Collingwood, "The Limits of Historical Knowledge" [1928], quoted in W. J. Van Der Dussen, *History as a Science: The Philosophy of R. G. Collingwood* (New York: Springer, 1983), 34.

11. Dorothy Ross, *The Origins of American Social Science* (New York: Cambridge University Press, 1990), 3.

12. Thompson, *An Inquiry into the Principles of the Distribution of Wealth*, iii.

13. Ross, *Origins of American Social Science*, 402.

14. Thomas C. Cochran, "The Presidential Synthesis in American History," *American Historical Review* 53 (July 1948), 748–59; Richard Hofstadter, "History and the Social Sciences," in Stern, ed., *The Varieties of History*, 359–70.

15. Eric R. Wolf, *Europe and the People Without History* (Berkeley: University of California Press, 1982), 8, 10.

16. Norman J.G. Pounds, *A Historical Geography of Europe, 1500–1840* (Cambridge: Cambridge University Press, 1979), 6.

17. Richard J. Smith, *Chinese Maps: Images of All Under Heaven* (Oxford: Oxford University Press, 1996), 7, 63.

18. Ellsworth Huntington, *The Principles of Human Geography* (New York: Wiley, 1922), 58, 60, 387.

19. Frederick Jackson Turner, *The Frontier in American History* (New York: Holt, 1920), 34, 322–23.

20. Theodore Roosevelt, *The Winning of the West* (New York: Putnam, 1889), 1: Foreword; Frederick Jackson Turner, *The Rise of the New West, 1819–1829* (New York: Harper, 1904), xix; Thomas G. Dyer, *Theodore Roosevelt and the Idea of Race* (Baton Rouge: Louisiana State University Press, 1992), 54; Ray Allen Billington, *Frederick Jackson Turner* (New York: Oxford University Press, 1973), 497.

21. Donald Meinig, *The Shaping of America: A Geographical Perspective on 500 Years of History, Vol. 2: Continental America, 1800–1867* (New Haven, Conn.: Yale University Press, 1995), 558; Alfred Crosby, *The Columbian Exchange* [1972] (rev. ed. New York: Praeger, 2003), 37.

22. Frank J. Goodnow, "The Work of the American Political Science Association," Presidential Address 1903, *Proceedings of the American Political Science Association* 1 (1903), 41.

23. John A. Garraty, *The Nature of Biography* (New York: Knopf, 1957), 195; James MacGregor Burns, *Transforming Leadership: The Pursuit of Happiness* (New York: Atlantic Monthly Press, 2003), 2. I co-edit for the University Press of Kansas a series of legal histories somewhat boldly entitled Landmark Law Cases and American Society. Our authors include historians and political scientists, among others. While a practiced eye can tell the difference in approach and emphasis between the historians and the political scientists, a high standard of historical research characterizes both groups' work.

24. Peter Johns, "Quantitative Methods," in David Marsh and Gerry Stokes, eds., *Theory and Methods in Political Science* (3rd ed. London: Palgrave, 2010), 268–69; David Sanders, "Behavioural Analysis," ibid., 30–31; Vivien Lowndes, "The Institutional Approach," ibid., 64; Brian Balogh, *A Government Out of Sight: The Mystery of National Authority in Nineteenth-Century America* (New York: Cambridge University Press, 2008), 312; Williamjames Hull Hoffer, *To Enlarge the Machinery of Government: Congressional Debates and the Growth of the American State, 1858–1891* (Baltimore: Johns Hopkins University Press, 2007), 220, n.85; Stephen

Skowronek, *Building an American State: The Expansion of National Administrative Capacities, 1877–1920* (New York: Cambridge University Press, 1982).

25. David Hume, *Essays Moral and Philosophical*, in *The Philosophical Works of David Hume* (Boston: Little, Brown, 1854), 3:28.

26. On upstreaming, see Daniel Richter, *Facing East from Indian Country: A Native History of Early America* (Cambridge, Mass.: Harvard University Press, 2001), 14–15; and Richard White, *The Middle Ground: Indians, Empires, and Republics in the Great Lakes Region, 1650–1815* (New York: Cambridge University Press, 1991), xiv.

27. Josiah Nott and George Giddon, *Types of Mankind* (Philadelphia: Lippincott, 1855), 457, 460. On the utility of Nott's work for the defense of slavery, see Eric McKitrick, *Slavery Defended* (Englewood Cliffs, N.J.: Prentice Hall, 1963), 126.

28. Ruth Benedict, *The Chrysanthemum and the Sword: Patterns of Japanese Culture* (Boston: Houghton, Mifflin, 1946), 7, 307–8; C. Douglas Lummis, quoted in Pauline Kent, "Misconceived Configurations of Ruth Benedict: The Debate in Japan over *The Chrysanthemum and the Sword*," in Dolores E. Janiewski and Lois Banner, eds., *Reading Benedict/Reading Mead: Feminism, Race, and Imperial Visions* (Baltimore: Johns Hopkins University Press, 2004), 183–84.

29. Clifford Geertz, *The Interpretation of Cultures* [1973] (rev. ed. New York: Basic Books, 1973), 10, 362; Burrow, *The History of Histories*, 462–63; Rhys Isaac, "On Explanation, Text, and Terrifying Power in Ethnographic History," *Yale Journal of Criticism: Interpretation in the Humanities* 6 (1993), 217–36.

30. Richard Hofstadter, *Social Darwinism in American Thought* (rev. ed. Boston: Beacon, 1992), 51–66.

31. William Graham Sumner, *Folkways: A Study in the Sociological Importance of Usages, Manners, Customs, Mores, and Morals* (Boston: Ginn, 1906), 38, 170; Sumner, *The Forgotten Man and Other Essays* [1910] (reprinted Manchester, N.H.: Ayer, 1969), 170.

32. Edward A. Ross, *Foundations of Sociology* (New York: Macmillan, 1905), 73, 82, 191–92.

33. Ross, *Seventy Years of It: An Autobiography* (New York: Appleton-Century, 1936), 233; Daniel J. Kevles, *In the Name of Eugenics: Genetics and the Uses of Human Heredity* (Berkeley: University of California Press, 1985), 101.

34. Mark C. Carnes, *Reacting to the Past Series Pedagogy Manual* privately printed (copy at University of Georgia Reacting to the Past program); Talcott Parsons, *The Social System* [1951] (London: Routledge, 1991), 95.

35. Herbert Hovenkamp, summarizing Wayland's philosophy, in *Enterprise and American Law* (Cambridge, Mass.: Harvard University Press, 1991), 75.

36. Richard T. Ely, *The Social Law of Service* (New York: Eaton and Mains, 1896), 52, 58, 130, 149–50.

37. Robert William Fogel and Stanley L. Engerman, *Time on the Cross: The Economics of American Negro Slavery* (Boston: Little, Brown, 1974), 4.

38. Herbert G. Gutman and Richard Sutch, "The Slave Family" in Paul A. David et al., eds., *Reckoning with Slavery* (New York: Oxford University Press, 1976), 96.
39. Peter Burke, *History and Social Theory* (Ithaca, N.Y.: Cornell University Press, 1992), 114.
40. Sigmund Freud, *Moses and Monotheism* [1937], trans. Katherine Jones (New York: Vintage, 1967), 152–53.
41. Erik Erikson, *Young Man Luther: A Study in Psychoanalysis and History* (New York: Norton, 1958), 251–52.
42. Jacques Barzun, *Clio and the Doctors: Psycho-history, Quanto-history, and History* (Chicago: University of Chicago Press, 1974), 15; Philip Greven, *The Protestant Temperament: Patterns of Child-Rearing, Religious Experience, and the Self in Early America* (New York: Knopf, 1977), 15; Peter Gay, *Freud for Historians* (New York: Oxford University Press, 1986), 205, 206.
43. Robert Jervis, *Perception and Misperception in International Politics* (Princeton, N.J.: Princeton University Press, 1976), 384; Allan R. Buss and Wayne Poley, *Individual Differences: Traits and Factors* (New York: Wiley, 1976), 13. On trait scaling, see, e.g., Peter C. Hoffer, N. E. H. Hull, and Steven L. Allen, "Choosing Sides: A Quantitative Study of the Psychological Determinants of Political Affiliation," *Journal of American History* 65 (1978), 344–66; and Hoffer, "Psychohistory and Empirical Group Affiliation," *Journal of Interdisciplinary History* 9 (1978), 131–45.

Notes to Chapter 4

1. John Clive, *Not by Fact Alone: Essays on the Writing and Reading of History* (Boston: Houghton Mifflin, 1989), 298; Frederic William Maitland, *A Sketch of English Legal History* (New York: Putnam, 1915), 3; Henry Adams, *The Education of Henry Adams* (Boston: Houghton Mifflin, 1918), 499–500; James Goodman, "History as Creative Writing," March 22, 2010, History News Network, www.hnn.us/articles/124629.html. Spoiler alert: Anonymous referees of my work have sometimes accused me of trying to emulate some of the older stylists I praise in this chapter, not intending the comment as a compliment. But I am honored by the comparison.
2. Marcia R. Pointon and Lucy Peltz, *History of Art: A Student's Handbook* (London: Psychology Press, 1997), 81; Dominick Lacapra, on Sartre and history, *Rethinking Intellectual History* (Ithaca, N.Y.: Cornell University Press, 1983), 217.
3. Howard Doughty, *Francis Parkman* (Cambridge, Mass.: Harvard University Press, 1983), 142 and after.
4. Francis Parkman, *Montcalm and Wolfe* [1884] (Boston: Little, Brown, 1914) 1: 362.
5. Francis Parkman, *The Jesuits in North America* [1867], in Samuel Eliot Morison, ed., *The Parkman Reader* (Boston: Little, Brown, 1955), 26, 30, 38, 52, 41.
6. David Arthur Hughes [1914], *Thomas Babington Macaulay the Rhetorician: An Examination of His Structural Devices in the History of England* (Ithaca, N.Y.:

Cornell University Press, 2009), 3. The entire treatise is devoted to Macaulay's sentence structure.

7. Thomas Babington Macaulay, *The History of England from the Accession of James II* [1848] (London: Dent, 1907), 1:615.

8. Clive, *Not by Fact Alone*, 67.

9. Stephen Ambrose, *Undaunted Courage: Meriwether Lewis, Thomas Jefferson, and the Opening of the American West* (New York: Simon and Schuster, 1996), 405; Ambrose, *Citizen Soldiers: The U.S. Army from the Normandy Beaches to the Bulge to the Surrender of Germany* (New York: Simon and Schuster, 1998), 159; Hoffer, *Past Imperfect*, 176–97.

10. David McCullough, *John Adams* (New York: Simon and Schuster, 2001), 18. Shelby Foote's *The Civil War: A Narrative* (3v., New York: Random House, 1974) remains a bestseller more than a quarter-century after its first publication.

11. Arthur M. Schlesinger Jr., *A Thousand Days: John F. Kennedy in the White House* (Boston: Houghton Mifflin, 1965), 92.

12. Dennis Maclean, "Influential Historian, Intellectual, Aide to President Kennedy," March 1, 2007, *Los Angeles Times*, articles.latimes.com/2007/mar/01/nation/na-schlesinger1.

13. Daniel Boorstin, *The Seekers: The Story of Man's Continuing Quest to Understand His World* (New York: Random House, 1998), 1.

14. Robert D. McFadden, "Daniel Boorstin, 89, Former Librarian of Congress, Dies," *New York Times* March 1, 2004, A1.

15. Irving Stone, "Afterword," *Lust for Life: The Story of Vincent Van Gogh* [1934] (New York: Longmans, 1935), 487.

16. Eric Foner, "Who Owns History?" kwls.org/lit/podcasts/2009/03/eric_foner_2009_who_owns_histo.cfm; John Demos, *The Unredeemed Captive: A Family Story from Early America* (New York: Knopf, 1994), 189–90.

17. Demos, "In Search of Reasons for Historians to Read Novels," *American Historical Review* 103 (December 1998), 1527 poses the novelistic alternative.

18. Carlo Ginzburg, *The Cheese and the Worms: The Cosmos of a Sixteenth Century Miller*, trans. John Tedeschi (Baltimore: Johns Hopkins University Press, 1992), 2.

19. T. H. Breen, *Imagining the Past: East Hampton Histories* (Athens: University of Georgia Press, 1996), 14, 15; and Daniel K. Richter, *Facing East from Indian Country: A Native History of Early America* (Cambridge, Mass.: Harvard University Press, 2001), 9, 13.

20. Laurel Thatcher Ulrich, *A Midwife's Tale: The Life of Martha Ballard, Based on Her Diary, 1785–1812* (New York: Knopf, 1991), 33; Martha Hodes, "Experimental History in the Classroom," AHA *Perspectives* 45 (May 2007), 38.

21. Elizabeth A. Clark, *History, Theory, Text: Historians and the Linguistic Turn* (Cambridge, Mass.: Harvard University Press, 2004), 131; Willie Thompson, "Postmodernism and Historiography" in Yerxa, ed., *Historical Thinking*, 69–73. I suppose that adopting deconstruction means never having to spend a week inhaling dust

and mold in an archive, surely a plus for intellectual historians but hardly a basis for defending the method.

22. John E. Toews, "Intellectual History After the Linguistic Turn," *American Historical Review* 92 (1987), 880, 881; Keith Jenkins, *Re-Thinking History* (London: Routledge, 1991), 60–61. Jenkins goes beyond this. "The historian's referent is 'nothing' but the product of their [*sic*] inferences based upon their existential (personal, ethical, public ideological . . .) condition." Jenkins, *At the Limits of History: Essays on Theory and Practice* (London: Routledge, 2009), 263.

23. Joyce Appleby, "One Good Turn Deserves Another: Moving Beyond the Linguistic Turn," *American Historical Review* 94 (December 1989), reprinted in Appleby, *A Restless Past: History and the American Public* (Lanham, Md.: Rowman and Littlefield, 2005), 123.

24. Keith Windschuttle, *The Killing of History: How Literary Critics and Social Theorists Are Murdering Our Past* (New York: Free Press, 1996), 227, 239; Hayden White, *Metahistory* (Baltimore: Johns Hopkins University Press, 1973), 12. Of course, one might refute White by asking if he has a history that is anything more than literary trope. The answer is yes—of course—trivially so. Like Samuel Johnson's kicking the stone to refute Bishop George Berkeley's philosophy (the only thing we can know is what is in our perceptual experience), so one disproves White by asking him to tell us about his life.

Notes to Chapter 5

1. Allan Nevins, *The Gateway to History* (New York: Doubleday, 1962), 335, 348; Paul Murray Kendall, "Walking the Boundaries," in Stephen Oates, ed., *Biography as High Adventure: Life-Writers Speak on Their Art* (Amherst: University of Massachusetts Press, 1986), 32; Peter France and William St. Claire, *Mapping Lives: The Uses of Biography* (New York: Oxford University Press, 2004), 130–32, 330.

2. Mary Antin, *The Promised Land* [1912], quoted in Stephan Thernstrom, *The Other Bostonians: Poverty and Progress in the American Metropolis, 1880–1970* (Cambridge, Mass.: Harvard University Press, 1973), 1.

3. Ulrich, *A Midwife's Tale*, 33.

4. Ralph Waldo Emerson, "The Uses of Great Men," in Emerson, *Addresses and Lectures* (Boston: Houghton Mifflin, 1883), 9; Thomas Carlyle, "Of Heroes and Hero Worship," *Works of Thomas Carlyle* (London: Chapman and Hall, 1869), 12:285.

5. John Milton Cooper Jr., "Conception, Conversation, and Comparison: My Experiences as a Biographer," in Lloyd E. Ambrosius, ed., *Writing Biography: Historians and Their Craft* (Lincoln: University of Nebraska Press, 2004), 81.

6. Philip Stadter, "Introduction," *Plutarch and the Historical Tradition* (London: Routledge, 1992), 1.

7. *Plutarch's Lives*, tr. John Dryden, ed. Arthur Hugh Clough (New York: Modern Library, 2001), 2:236.

8. Ibid., 2:443.

9. An apology of sorts: Social historians and readers who think social history is far more important than traditional historical subjects are not going to be happy with my focus on greatness. This is one of the dangers of the synedochal approach—choosing one subject of the many one might elect from biography to explore the connection between biography and history. But my defense is that biography grew out of the biographers' attempt to understand greatness.

10. Samuel Eliot Morison, *Admiral of the Ocean Sea: A Life of Christopher Columbus* (Boston: Little, Brown, 1942), 6.

11. George H.W. Bush, Proclamation, in John Yewell, Chris Dodger, and Jan DeSirey, eds., *Confronting Columbus: An Anthology* (Jefferson, N.C.: McFarland, 1992), 200.

12. American Library Association Resolution, in *Confronting Columbus*, 196; *Newsday*, October 14, 1991, 44. See Hoffer, *Past Imperfect* (New York: PublicAffairs Press, 2004), 95–96, for the full text of these documents.

13. Donald F. Lach, *Asia in the Making of Europe* (Chicago: University of Chicago Press, 1977), 448, 456.

14. Daniel Boorstin, *The Discoverers* (New York: Random House, 1985), 252, 253.

15. Morison, *Admiral of the Ocean Sea*, 468.

16. Alfred W. Crosby, *The Columbian Exchange: The Biological and Cultural Consequences of 1492* (2nd ed. Westport, Conn.: Greenwood, 2003), 31 and after.

17. Kirkpatrick Sale, *Christopher Columbus and the Conquest of Paradise* (New York: Knopf, 1990), 3.

18. James Johonnot, *The Ten Great Events in History* (New York: Appleton, 1887), 117. The Centennial Exposition was a success not only in attendance but also in conception—America was now a world leader in technology. But the Centennial also revealed a kind of anxiety among the moguls and the visionaries that the world was not so easily mastered as the array of exhibitions boasted. Bruno Giberti, *Designing the Centennial: A History of the 1876 International Exhibition in Philadelphia* (Lexington: University Press of Kentucky, 2002), 32.

19. Rossiter Johnson, "Parting Word," *The Great Events by Famous Historians: A comprehensive and readable account of the world's history, emphasizing the more important events, and presenting these as complete narratives in the master-words of the most eminent historians* (New York: The National Alumni, 1905–1914), 20: vii, viii.

20. Charles F. Horne, "An Outline Narrative of the Great Events," *Great Events* 1:27, 30, 31.

21. John Jay, "The Demand for Education in American History," American Historical Association presidential address, 1890, www.historians.org/info/AHA_History/jjay.htm.

22. Frank H. Severance, "Preface," in Arthur C. Parker, *The Life of General Ely S. Parker* (Buffalo, N.Y.: Buffalo Historical Society, 1919), xi.

23. Arthur M. Schlesinger, "Historians Rate the U.S. Presidents," *Life* (November 1, 1948), 65–66, 68, 73–74; Arthur M. Schlesinger Jr., "Our Presidents: A Rating by 75

Historians," *New York Times Magazine* (July 1962), 12–13, 40–41, 43; en.wikipedia.
org/wiki/Historical_rankings_of_United_States_Presidents. Is consensus an
approximation of objectivity? Francis Galton, an English statistician, proposed a
famous experiment—have the crowd at an English fair guess the weight of an ox
from looking at it. List their various guesses (the more the better) and find that
the median is very close to the actual weight of the ox. *The Life, Letters and Labors
of Francis Galton*, ed. Karl Pearson (Cambridge: Cambridge University Press,
1914), 2: 402–4.

24. Jefferson Davis, *The Rise and Fall of the Confederate Government* (New York:
Appleton, 1881) 2:180, 586; Stephen Douglas, 1858, quoted in William Gardner, *The
Life of Stephen A. Douglas* (Boston: Roxburgh, 1905), 149; George S. McGovern,
Abraham Lincoln (New York: Farrar, Straus & Giroux, 2008), 1, 2; Michael Burlin-
game, *The Inner World of Abraham Lincoln* (Urbana: University of Illinois Press,
1997), 94, 95; Carl Sandburg, *Abraham Lincoln: The Prairie Years and the War Years*,
ed. Edward C. Goodman (New York: Sterling, 2007), 434. A nearly exhaustive
bibliography of the past forty years of Lincoln books appears in Matthew Pinsker,
"Lincoln Theme 2.0," *Journal of American History* 96 (September 2009), 417–40.
But why all these pages on Lincoln? The answer is because of the complexities of
the man, the varying assessments of him by historians, the way he is seen today
and is likely to be seen in the future. When I wrote these passages, Eric Foner had
not yet published his Pulitzer Prize–winning *The Fiery Trial: Abraham Lincoln and
American Slavery* (New York: Norton, 2010) nor John Witt his marvelous *Lincoln's
Code* (Cambridge, Mass.: Harvard University Press, 2012). I could add five or ten
more to that list. The reason I chose Lincoln is—who else could I have chosen?

25. Allen C. Guelzo, "The Not-So-Grand Review: Abraham Lincoln in the Journal of
American History," *Journal of American History* 96 (September 2009), 400; Mark
E. Neely Jr., *The Fate of Liberty: Lincoln and Civil Liberties* (New York: Oxford
University Press, 1991), 117. The prime detractors: James G. Randall, "The Blunder-
ing Generation," *Mississippi Valley Historical Review* 27 (1940), 3–28; Avery O.
Craven, "The 1840s and the Democratic Process," *Journal of Southern History* 16
(1950), 161–76.

26. James M. McPherson, *Abraham Lincoln* (New York: Oxford University Press,
2000), 62.

27. Note that Lincoln wrote his own speeches. He was a careful and thoughtful writer,
reworking his speeches many times. Other great speeches of modern presidents
were written by close advisors and "ghosts"—for example, the famous collaboration of Peggy Noonan, speechwriter, and President Ronald Reagan, dramatic
deliverer of Noonan's words. Of course, Noonan's memory sometimes plays tricks
about who said what. Robert Schlesinger, *White House Ghosts: Presidents and
Their Speechwriters* (New York: Simon and Schuster, 2008), 2, 344.

28. Garry Wills, *Lincoln at Gettyburg: The Words That Remade America* (New York:
Simon and Schuster, 1992), 146, 147.

29. Lincoln quoted in McPherson, *Lincoln*, 10.
30. Stephen Berry, *House of Abraham: Lincoln and the Todds, A Family Divided by War* (New York: Houghton Mifflin, 2007), 181.
31. Edna Green Medford, C-SPAN, "C-SPAN Releases Second Historians' Survey of Presidential Leadership," February 15, 2009, www.c-span.org/pdf/C-SPANpresidentialsurveyPR021509.pdf.
32. Okay—I know this comes awfully (in both senses of the word) close to various conceptualizations of "performativity"—words "do something in the world." But if past people are the sum of their words, that is not because of our nature; it is because of the nature of the primary sources historians use. See James Loxley, *Performativity* (London: Taylor and Francis, 2007), 2 and after.
33. Justin Kaplan, "The Real Life," in Oates, ed., *Biography as High Adventure*, 71.

Notes to Chapter 6

1. On the "prisoner's dilemma," Alex Abella, *Soldiers of Reason: The RAND Corporation and the Rise of the American Empire* (New York: Houghton Mifflin, 2009), 54–55, 92; Peter Charles Hoffer, *The Historians' Paradox: A Philosophy of History for Our Times* (New York: New York University Press, 2008), 138–41. We confront one form or another of the prisoner's dilemma every day. The best-known version is the one on the police procedural television show, in fact the one that Albert Tucker, a mathematician at Princeton University, used to introduce the game to his students in the early 1950s. The police have arrested and brought to the station house two or more suspects for the same offense. They put each in a separate interrogation room and tell each one, "Here is a one-time offer. The first of you to take it will get a guaranteed reduced sentence. You have to agree to testify against the others. If they take it first, you will do a long stretch in the penitentiary." If no one talks, the police will not be able to charge anyone with anything. But each suspect cannot know what the others will do. A suspect who stays silent while another agrees to the deal is the big loser. Cooperation with the police seems to offer the best outcome, called the dominant choice, and seems to be the rational one. But the best outcome for both suspects is to say nothing, or deny everything. Then both walk out of the station. The trick is that the rational decision for one player is the irrational one for both.
2. Daniel C. McCool, *Public Policy Theories, Models, and Concepts* (Englewood Cliffs, N.J.: Prentice Hall, 1995), 3, 8; William N. Dunne, *Public Policy Analysis: An Introduction* (Upper Saddle River, N.J.: Prentice Hall, 2008), 467.
3. George Santayana, *The Life of Reason, Volume One* [1905] (Teddington: Echo, 2006), 131.
4. Judith Stiehm, *The U.S. Army War College: Military Education in a Democracy* (Philadelphia: Temple University Press, 2002), 34, 36, 111, 121; Colin S. Gray, "The American Way of War," in Anthony D. McIvor, ed., *Rethinking the Principles of War* (Annapolis: Naval Institute Press, 2005), 13–40; Antulio J. Echevarria II,

"American Strategic Culture: Problems and Prospects," in Hew Strachan and Sibylle Scheipers, eds., *The Changing Character of War* (New York: Oxford University Press, 2007), 431–45.

5. Harold Lasswell, *Power and Personality* (New York: Norton, 1948), 123; John A. Lynn, *Battle: A History of Combat and Culture* (New York: Basic, 2003), 192–93 and after.

6. Carl von Clausewitz, *On War*, trans. Peter Paret (New York: Knopf, 1993), 69, 34.

7. Konrad Lorenz, *On Aggression* (2nd ed. London: Routledge, 2002), 259, 262.

8. Bartolomé de las Casas, *The Devastation of the Indies*, trans. Herma Briffault (Baltimore: Johns Hopkins University Press, 1992), 29.

9. John Fabian Witt, *Lincoln's Code: The Laws of War in American History* (New York: Free Press, 2012), 98, 119; Curtin, *The World and the West*, 22, 195–231.

10. John Keegan, *The History of War* (rev. ed. New York: Vintage, 1994), 4.

11. Colin Calloway, *One Vast Winter Count: The Native American West Before Lewis and Clark* (Lincoln: University of Nebraska Press, 2003), 230.

12. Theodore Roosevelt, *The Winning of the West* (New York: Putnam, 1889), 1:323; David E. Stannard, *American Holocaust: Columbus and the Conquest of the New World* (New York: Oxford University Press, 1992), 134.

13. *The Iliad*, tr. Adam Roberts (Ware: Wordsworth, 1995), bk. 7, lines 30–35; Susan Mattern, *Rome and the Enemy: Imperial Strategy in the Principate* (Berkeley: University of California Press, 1999), 10–11.

14. Augustine and Aquinas quoted in R. W. Dyson, *Aquinas, Political Writings* (Cambridge: Cambridge University Press, 2000), 240–41.

15. J. H. Elliott, *Empires of the Atlantic World: Britain and Spain in America, 1492–1830* (New Haven, Conn.: Yale University Press, 2005), 11.

16. William L. Shirer, *The Rise and Fall of the Third Reich* (New York: Simon and Schuster, 1960), 234; Benjamin Schwartz, "Hitler's Co-Conspirators," *Atlantic Monthly*, May 2009, online at www.theatlantic.com/doc/200905/nazi-germany; Richard M. Lerner, *Final Solutions: Biology, Prejudice, and Genocide* (State College: Pennsylvania State University Press, 2008), 80.

17. Witt, *Lincoln's Code*, 343–53.

18. Michael Walzer, *Just and Unjust Wars: A Moral Argument with Historical Illustrations* (New York: Basic Books, 1977), 36; Carl von Clausewitz, *On War*, 707.

19. The "good war"—sometimes used ironically, sometimes openly condemned, see, e.g., Studs Terkel, comp., *The Good War: An Oral History of World War II* (New York: Pantheon, 1984); Jacques R. Pauwels, *The Myth of the Good War: America in the Second World War* (New York: Lorimer, 2002), concludes that World War II was not fought for idealistic reasons because it left the colonial empires of the victors intact.

20. David M. Kennedy, *Freedom from Fear: The American People in Depression and War, 1929–1945* (New York: Oxford University Press, 2000), 465.

21. Ibid., 846, 847.

22. Tom Brokaw, *The Greatest Generation* (New York: Random House, 2004), 1; Peter Leese, *Shell Shock: Traumatic Neurosis and the British Soldiers of the First World War* (London: Palgrave, 2002), 56, 57, 115; Edgar Jones, *Shell Shock to PTSD: Military Psychiatry from 1900 to the Gulf War* (London: Psychology Press, 2006), 19; Gary S. Patton, "Generals Share Their Experience with PTSD," March 7, 2009, at www.cnn.com/2009/HEALTH/03/06/generals.ptsd/index.html.

23. Thomas E. Ricks, *Fiasco: The American Military Adventure in Iraq* (New York: Penguin, 2006), 193.

24. James C. Blight, "Is Afghanistan Obama's Vietnam?" *The Chronicle Review* February 27, 2009, B12–B13.

25. Joseph Stiglitz and Linda Bilmes, "Hidden Wounds and Accounting Tricks: Disguising the True Costs," in Miriam Pemberton and William D. Hartung, eds., *Lessons from Iraq: Avoiding the Next War* (Boulder, Colo.: Paradigm, 2008), 48–64.

26. Ali A. Alawi, *The Occupation of Iraq: Winning the War, Losing the Peace* (New Haven, Conn.: Yale University Press, 2007), 13, 447–52.

27. George McGovern anecdote quoted in Miriam Pemberton, "Introduction," *Lessons from Iraq*, 1.

28. Frank Rich, *The Greatest Story Ever Sold: The Decline and Fall of Truth from 9/11 to Katrina* (New York: Penguin, 2006), 160.

29. William Tecumseh Sherman, letter 1865, quoted in B. H. Liddell Hart, *Sherman: Soldier, Realist, American* (New York: Dodd, Mead, 1929), 402; Gene Larocque to Studs Terkel, from *The Good War* (1985), quoted in Howard Zinn, comp., *Voices of a People's History of the United States* (New York: Seven Stories Press, 2004), 374, 376.

30. Paul Kennedy, *The Rise and Fall of the Great Powers* (New York: Random House, 1987), 514–15.

31. Ibid., 439, 689.

32. Niall Ferguson, *Colossus: The Rise and Fall of the American Empire* (rev. ed. New York: Penguin, 2004), 20, 23, 300, 301, 302.

Notes to Chapter 7

1. Peter Charles Hoffer, *A Nation of Laws: America's Imperfect Pursuit of Justice* (Lawrence: University Press of Kansas, 2010), xiii. Portions of chapter 7 here are drawn from the text of this work.

2. Austin Sarat and Thomas Kearns, "Writing History and Registering Memory," in Sarat and Kearns, eds., *History, Memory, and the Law* (Ann Arbor: University of Michigan Press, 2002), 4.

3. Thomas Macintyre Cooley, *The General Principles of Constitutional Law in the United States of America* (Boston: Little, Brown, 1880), 82; the Langdellian or classical common law view in William LaPiana, *Logic and Experience: The Origin of Modern American Legal Education* (New York: Oxford University Press, 1994), 3; Oliver Wendell Holmes Jr., *The Common Law* (Boston: Little, Brown, 1881), 1. On

Holmes, Cooley, and the "singing" reason of the law, see William Wiecek, *The Lost World of Classical Legal Thought: Law and Ideology in America, 1886–1937* (New York: Oxford University Press, 2001), 7 and after.

4. Lawrence Friedman, *The History of American Law* (New York: Simon and Schuster, 1985), ix, xii; Lawrence M. Friedman, "Introduction," in *The Law and Society Reader*, ed. Lawrence M. Friedman, Stuart MacAulay, and John M. Stookey (New York: Norton, 1995), 2; Lawrence Friedman to the author, July 27, 2009; G. Edward White, *American Judicial Tradition* (3rd ed. New York: Oxford University Press, 2007), xx.

5. Elizabeth Mensch, "The History of Mainstream Legal Thought," in David Kairys, ed., *The Politics of Law: An Intellectual Critique* (3rd ed. New York: Basic, 1997), 1, 2.

6. Edward A. Purcell, *Originalism, Federalism, and the American Constitutional Enterprise: A Historical Inquiry* (New Haven, Conn.: Yale University Press, 2007), 176. The distinctions among original meaning and original intent are teased out in Jack Rakove, *Original Meanings: Politics and Ideas in the Making of the Constitution* (New York: Knopf, 1996), 7–8. See also James E. Ryan, "Does It Take a Theory? Originalism, Active Liberty, and Minimalism," *Stanford Law Review* 58 (March 2006), 1264. In 1985 Attorney General Edwin Meese's call for a "jurisprudence of original intent" before the American Bar Association was rebutted by Justice William Brennan's call for a living Constitution in a speech at Georgetown Law School. A "new originalism" has since emerged, relying less on the specific intent of the framers and instead on the plain meaning of the language at the time it was written. Justice Antonin Scalia has called this the basis for a "rock-solid, unchanging Constitution," a conclusion that the continuing debates over the history and the doctrine do little to support. Stephen G. Calabresi, in Antonin Scalia and Stephen G. Calabresi, eds., *Originalism: A Quarter Century of Debate* (New York: Regnery, 2007), 1; Antonin Scalia, *A Matter of Interpretation: Federal Courts and the Law* (Princeton, N.J.: Princeton University Press, 1997), 47. On the Meese–Brennan exchange, see Seth Stern and Stephen Wermiel, *Justice Brennan: Liberal Champion* (New York: Houghton Mifflin, 2010), 504–506. Both of the speeches appear in Scalia and Calabresi, eds., *Originalism: A Quarter Century of Debate*, 47–71. On the "new originalism" and its problems, see Mark Tushnet, "*Heller* and the New Originalism," 69 *Ohio State Law Journal* (2008), 609–610, and R. B. Bernstein, "The Constitution as an Exploding Cigar and other 'Historians' Heresies' About a Constitutional Orthodoxy," *New York Law Review* 55 (2010/2011), 1073–1095.

7. Alan Watson, *Failure of the Legal Imagination* (Philadelphia: University of Pennsylvania Press, 1987), 107; Bernard Schwartz, *The Law in America: A History* (New York: McGraw-Hill, 1974), vii; Karl N. Llewellyn, *The Common Law Tradition: Deciding Appeals* (Boston: Little, Brown, 1960), 36.

8. Ann Curthoys, Ann Genovese, and Alex Reilly, *Rights and Redemption: History, Law, and Indigenous People* (Seattle: University of Washington Press, 2008), 16. A

less-than-friendly view of the mangling of history in the service of constitutional argument is Martin S. Flaherty, "History 'Lite' in Modern American Constitutionalism," *Columbia Law Review* 95 (1995), 523–90.

9. On the justice and the professor, see Leonard Levy, *The Emergence of a Free Press* (New York: Oxford University Press, 1985), xvii–xviii. For a more sympathetic version of the possibilities of judicial use of history, see William E. Nelson, "History and Neutrality in Constitutional Adjudication," *University of Virginia Law Review* 72 (1986), 1237–96.

10. On historians as expert witnesses, see Brian W. Martin, "Working with Lawyers: A Historians' Perspective," *OAH Newsletter* 30 (May 2002), 4–5; John A. Neuenschwander, "Historians as Expert Witnesses: The View from the Bench," *OAH Newsletter* (August 2002), 1–6; Patricia Cohen, "History for Hire in Industrial Lawsuits," *New York Times*, June 14, 2003, B7–8; and Peter Charles Hoffer and N. E. H. Hull, "Historians and the Impeachment Imbroglio: In Search of a Serviceable History," *Rutgers Law Journal* 31 (2000), 473–90.

11. J. Morgan Kousser, "Are Expert Witnesses Whores? Reflections on Objectivity and Scholarship in Expert Witnessing," *Public Historian* 6 (1984), 7, 6; Jonathan D. Martin, "Historians at the Gate: Accommodating Expert Historical Testimony in Federal Courts," *New York University Law Review* 78 (October 2003), 1524; the Kelly and Rothman quotations are from Curthoys, Genovese, and Reilly, *Rights*, 19, 16; Rothman, "Serving Clio and the Client," the Garrison Lecture, April 26, 2002, *Bulletin of the History of Medicine* 77 (2003), 44.

12. Douglas R. Littlefield, "A Different Kind of History: Historians in the Legal Arena," talk at Organization of American Historians convention, April 20, 2012.

13. This is a very simplified version of a pretty complex subject. For more, see Peter Charles Hoffer, *The Law's Conscience: Equitable Constitutionalism in America* (Chapel Hill: University of North Carolina Press, 1990), 7–21.

14. Edward D. Re, *Remedies: Cases and Materials* (Mineola, N.Y.: Foundation Press, 1983), 683.

15. Alfred Brophy, *Reparations: Pro and Con* (New York: Oxford University Press, 2006), 40–45; Peter Irons, *Justice at Law: The Story of the Japanese-American Internment Cases* (rev. ed. Berkeley: University of California Press, 1993), tells the story of the original cases and the suits for reparations.

16. American Jewish Historical Society, *American Jewish Desk Reference* (New York: Random House, 1999), 30.

17. www.usatoday.com/news/world/2007-11-22-israel-germany_N.htm.

18. Peter Charles Hoffer, *For Ourselves and Our Posterity: The Preamble to the Federal Constitution in American History* (New York: Oxford University Press, 2012), 59–64.

19. Robert E. Keeton, *Judging* (St. Paul, Minn.: West, 1990), 15; Prigg v. Pennsylvania 41 U.S. 539, 610 (1841) (Story J.). Story letter quoted in Robert Cover, *Justice Accused: Anti-Slavery and the Judicial Process* (New Haven, Conn.: Yale University Press, 1984), 119.

20. Brown University Media Relations, "Slavery and Justice: Background on the Report—Not the Last Words, but the First Words in a Continuing Dialogue" October 18, 2006; brown.edu/Administration/News_Bureau/2006-07/06-037b. html.

21. "Slavery and Justice," Report of the Brown University Steering Committee on Slavery and Justice, October 2006, brown.edu/Research/Slavery_Justice/report.

22. Sarat and Kearns, "Writing History and Registering Memory," 9.

Notes to the Conclusion

1. MacMillan, *Dangerous Games*, 35; Laurel Thatcher Ulrich quoted in Matthew Price, "Hollow History," *Boston Globe*, October 24, 2004, E1; Eric Foner, *Who Owns History? Rethinking the Past in a Changing World* (New York: Hill and Wang, 2002), xix.

2. American Historical Association, *Statement on Standards of Professional Conduct* Approved by Professional Division, December 9, 2004, and adopted by Council, January 6, 2005; historians.org/pubs/Free/ProfessionalStandards.cfm. Full disclosure: I was on the Professional Division of the AHA when we revised the standards. The primary draftsman was William Cronon. Bill strongly felt that the document should not have a named author, as it represented the views of the AHA. For the vice president of the division, this seems a correct view. But given that it was a historical document written at a time and place by real people, not only do its authors deserve mention, but future historians should demand that the authorship of the document be recorded.

3. Plumb, *Death of the Past*, 110.

4. John Lukacs, "Putting Man Before Descartes," *American Scholar* Winter 2009, www.theamericanscholar.org/putting-man-before-descartes; Hoffer, *Historians' Paradox*, 182.

5. Keith Jenkins, *Re-thinking History*, 19. Jenkins believes that history is fundamentally ideology masquerading as knowledge and wants history to "lose its innocence" by becoming "skeptical." Ibid., 68–69. My reply—think things, not words. Oliver Wendell Holmes Jr., "Law in Science and Science in Law," *Harvard Law Review* 12 (1899), 460.

6. Swabey, *Judgment of History*, 251, 252; Carl Becker quoted in Joyce Appleby, *A Restless Past*, 133; John Hope Franklin quoted in Andrew L. Yarrow, "John Hope Franklin, Scholar of African-American History, Is Dead at 94," *New York Times*, March 256, 2009, B13.

A VERY SHORT BIBLIOGRAPHY
(WITH ANNOTATIONS)

In one sense, the bibliography for this book is every history ever written. Alas, that sort of bibliography would not be of much use to anyone and would take up a lot of space. There's so much more to be said, but there is also a time to stop. As one of Robert Benchley's more outrageous characters told another in "Another Uncle Edith Christmas Story" (*The Benchley Round Up*, 1983), "If you don't shut up, I will keep right on with the story. You can't intimidate me."

The following is a very short and eclectic list of books on history and historical writing. Some are textbooks themselves. Some are classics. I have omitted the "how to" books for undergraduates writing history term papers and reader/anthologies. Here follows the list, with some comments of my own (recognizing that by the time this book reaches readers the list will be out of date).

Banner, James M. Jr., *Being a Historian: An Introduction to the Professional World of History*. New York: Cambridge University Press, 2012. Just what it advertises, an inside look at the work of public historians, academic historians, and historical organizations.

Barzun, Jacques, *Clio and the Doctors: Psycho-history, Quanto-history, and History*. Chicago: University of Chicago Press, 1974. A beautifully crafted and passionate defense of the literary tradition in history, bashing new methods along the way (a sort of academic "whack-a-mole").

Barzun, Jacques, and Henry Graff, *The Modern Researcher*, 6th ed. Belmont, Calif.: Wadsworth. 2003. The bible of methods for three generations of beginning history graduate students, but heavy going for the uninitiated.

Breen, T. H., *Imagining the Past: East Hampton Histories*. Athens: University of Georgia Press, 1996. A lovely first-person essay on how to recover a community's past from under layers of myth, faulty memory, and self-promotion.

Breisach, Ernst, *On the Future of History: The Postmodern Challenge and Its Aftermath*. Chicago: University of Chicago Press, 2003. A balanced and learned treatise on history, linking the distant past to some of the most recent trends. Sometimes slow going, however.

———, *Historiography: Ancient, Medieval, and Modern*. 3rd ed. Chicago: University of Chicago Press, 2007. The *summa historiographica* (apologies to St. Aquinas) of the Western tradition, but already out of date.

Burke, Peter, *History and Social Theory*. Ithaca, N.Y.: Cornell University Press, 1992. A very lively essay by a leading cultural historian on the eve of the invasion of literary criticism.

Burrow, John, *A History of Histories*. New York: Random House, 2009. A magisterial work, full of mature judgments and revealing anecdotes. The man can write, too.

Clark, Elizabeth A., *History, Theory, Text: Historians and the Linguistic Turn*. Cambridge, Mass.: Harvard University Press, 2004. Infused (and suffused) with the new literary turn in historical writing. Not for the squeamish when it comes to jargon.

Clive, John, *Not by Fact Alone: Essays on the Writing and Reading of History*. Boston: Houghton Mifflin, 1989. A collection of essays that is required reading in my opinion whether one cares about Thomas Babington Macaulay or not—in short, a literary treasure.

D'Arcy, M. C., *History: A Christian View*. New York: Farrar, Straus & Giroux, 1959. A learned and liberal essay in a way that, alas, now seems almost antique.

Day, Mark, *The Philosophy of History: An Introduction*. London: Continuum, 2008. A very simple, straightforward introduction to the subject, heavily flavored by English examples.

Elton, G. R., *The Practice of History*. London: Metheun, 1967. This is a classic of objectivist historical special pleading (whatever that means). Elton thought that with enough concern for one's sources' fallibility and one's own limitations, one could get the story right.

Evans, Richard J., *In Defense of History*. New York: Norton, 2000. A combination of cautions and examples of missteps whose purpose is not to bury historians but to praise them.

Foner, Eric, *Who Owns History? Rethinking the Past in a Changing World*. New York: Hill and Wang, 2002. Foner's own life in history, a very interesting one, combined with previously published essays and reviews.

Garraty, John A., *The Nature of Biography*. New York: Knopf, 1957. A timeless musing by a well-respected biographer. Garraty wrote one of the most popular textbooks in American history (now in its *n*th edition in the hands of Mark Carnes), and the skill needed to marshal so many facts for the textbook carried over into the essay on biography.

Gilderhus, Mark T., *History and Historians: A Historiographical Introduction*. 7th ed. Upper Saddle River, N.J.: Prentice Hall, 2010. A popular textbook for the newcomer to the subject.

Handlin, Oscar, *Truth in History*. Cambridge, Mass.: Harvard University Press, 1978. An elegant screed, if such an animal exists in the natural realm, by one of the most prolific and respected social historians of his day. Handlin, like Elton, thought that history could be too easily perverted by authors' present-minded concerns.

Higham, John, *History: Professional Scholarship in America*. Baltimore: Johns Hopkins University Press, 1986. A short version of a longer, co-written work on the rise of the historical profession. Higham gets it right.

Hoffer, Peter Charles, *The Historians' Paradox: A Philosophy of History for Our Times*. New York: New York University Press, 2008. A witty and provocative essay arguing that history is possible after all.

———, *Past Imperfect*. rev. ed. New York: PublicAffairs Press, 2007. A catalogue of historians' controversies, written in high dudgeon by a concerned student of historical methods that seems to have found an audience (if sales figures are correct) among equally concerned teachers of historical methods.

Iggers, George G., *Historiography in the Twentieth Century: From Scientific Objectivity to the Postmodern Challenge*. New York: Berg, 1991. A German scholarship–centered version of the story, beginning in the nineteenth century.

Jenkins, Keith, *Re-Thinking History*. London: Routledge, 1991. The first of Jenkins's series of books on the subject, arguing variously that there is no way to know what happened in the past and that the profession of history is pulling the wool over everyone's eyes. The fervor of the argument and the telling use of anecdotes almost convince one that Jenkins is right.

MacMillan, Margaret, *Dangerous Games: The Uses and Abuses of History*. New York: Modern Library, 2008. A series of dos and don'ts for historians, stitched together in attractive fashion.

Nevins, Allen, *The Gateway to History*. rev. ed. Garden City, N.Y.: Doubleday, 1962. My father's favorite book on history by the most prolific historian of his day. A journalist by training, an indefatigable researcher often employing squadrons of graduate assistants, and a lively writer, Nevins befriended every one of his biographical subjects. No muckraking here!

Novick, Peter, *That Noble Dream: The 'Objectivity Question' and the American Historical Profession*. New York: Cambridge University Press, 1988. A narrative of the rise and fall of historical profession spiced by delightfully wicked tales from the archives. Another required reading for beginning graduate students.

Plumb, J. H., *The Death of the Past*. 2nd ed. London: Palgrave, 2004. Part elegy, part lament, part personal narrative, all well within the English university tradition of grand history.

Rutland, Robert Allen, *Leading Historians of the United States, 1945–2000*. Columbia: University of Missouri Press, 2000. A collection of essays by—as promised—leading historians about their take on American historical scholarship. The contributors all belong, but one may question why some others, perhaps more deserving and certainly more diverse in their backgrounds, were not included.

Shapiro, Barbara, *A Culture of Fact: England, 1550–1720.* Ithaca, N.Y.: Cornell University Press, 2000. Shapiro's learned essay is the capstone of a life's investigation of early modern British thought. Here the subject is the origins of modern historical writing.

Stanford, Michael, *An Introduction to the Philosophy of History.* New York: Wiley, 1998. I had to include some academic philosophy of history in this list, and it might as well be this remarkably clear rendering of an otherwise opaque subject.

Stern, Fritz, ed., *The Varieties of History.* New York: Meridian, 1956. My introduction to the many faces of history, a collection of the greats of Western historical writing. Very dated now, I suppose, and hardly diverse, but still a handy introduction to the main themes of Columbia University's famous Western Civilization program.

Swabey, Marie, *The Judgment of History.* New York: Philosophical Library, 1954. An answer to the Marxist threat to liberal historical understandings. Today, more a primary source on the Cold War than a secondary source on historical writing.

Tosh, John, *The Pursuit of History.* 5th ed. New York: Longman, 2010. The most popular modern textbook on historical writing and methods. It gets bigger with each edition, the latest with marginal identifications and definitions, making it look more and more like a survey course textbook.

White, Hayden, *Metahistory: The Historical Imagination in Nineteenth-Century Europe.* Baltimore: Johns Hopkins University Press, 1973. The first of a series of increasingly provocative essays on the literary basis of all historical writing, and the target of many critics. White's brilliance and perverseness show through every page. A true showman's effort.

Windschuttle, Keith, *The Killing of History: How Literary Critics and Social Theorists Are Murdering Our Past.* New York: Free Press, 1996. An unrelenting attack on Hayden White and all who sail with him, written with such verve that one almost forgives its venom.

Wood, Gordon, *The Purpose of the Past.* New York: Penguin, 2008. An American master takes on the task of reminding his juniors where their duties lie. A more generous version of Handlin's *Truth in History,* though Wood does not write from an Olympian perch.

Yerxa, Donald A., ed., *Recent Themes in Historical Thinking, Historians in Conversation.* Columbia: University of South Carolina Press, 2008. A collection of historians' musings on the literary turn and other subjects. Given the variety in the essays and the somewhat complex organization of the book, remarkably readable.

INDEX

ABOUT THE AUTHOR

Peter Charles Hoffer is Distinguished Research Professor of History at the University of Georgia. He has taught history at Harvard, Ohio State, Notre Dame, Brooklyn College, and the University of Georgia and specializes in historical methods, early American history, and legal history. He has written or co-written more than three dozen books and edited another twenty, including *The Historian's Paradox: The Study of History in Our Time* (NYU Press, 2008).